THE NEW WOMAN
AND THE VICTORIAN NOVEL

The New Woman
and the Victorian Novel

Gail Cunningham

BARNES & NOBLE
BOOKS
10 East 53d St., New York 10022
(a division of Harper & Row Publishers, Inc.)

First published 1978 by
THE MACMILLAN PRESS LTD
London and Basingstoke

Published in the U.S.A. 1978 by
HARPER & ROW PUBLISHERS, INC.
BARNES & NOBLE IMPORT DIVISION

Library of Congress Cataloging in Publication Data

Cunningham, Gail.
  The new woman and the Victorian novel.

  Bibliography: p.
  Includes index.
  1. English fiction — 19th century — History and
criticism. 2. Women in literature. 3. English
fiction — Women authors — History and criticism.
  I. Title.
PR878.W6C8   1978   823′.03   78–6179
ISBN 0–06–491347–3

For my Mother and Father

Contents

Acknowledgements

My thanks are due to a great many people who have, in various ways, helped in the preparation of this book: to Dennis Burden, who was a constant source of advice and encouragement during the time of my initial research; to Tom Paulin, for generously sharing the fruits of his investigations into Hardy manuscripts; to Peter Kemp, whose criticisms and suggestions have been invaluable; to Piers Pennington and Gill Gibson for their patience and care in scrutinising the typescript; and lastly to my husband, without whose practical and emotional help the book would never have been completed.

G.C.

Introduction

She flouts Love's caresses
Reforms ladies' dresses
And scorns the Man-Monster's tirade;
She seems scarcely human
This mannish New Woman
This Queen of the Blushless Brigade.[1]

In the last years of the nineteenth century the Victorian middle classes were subjected to what was probably the most profound of the many shocks they had received throughout the reign. The age of *fin-de-siècle* may have failed to culminate in the fin-du-globe, languorously desired by Dorian Gray, but it certainly produced a dramatic and thrilling end to the Victorian era and its supposed stability of values. It was a period in which everything could be challenged, a time of enthusiastic extremism and gleeful revolt, of posturing dandyism, absinthe-sipping and bourgeosie-shocking, when reputations could be made by an exquisitely expressed preference for green, or yellow, or purple over more conventionally approved colours. But it was also a period of deeply serious inquiry, of impassioned debate over central questions of moral and social behaviour which created acute anxiety in those who felt themselves to be witnessing the breakdown of the rules traditionally thought to hold society together. The froth and ferment which gave rise to the naughty nineties image were symptoms of a deeper malaise, reflected in the most popular pejoratives of the time – 'morbid', 'decadent', 'degenerate', 'neurotic'. It was widely believed that society was sick, probably with an infection spread from Europe through the new translations of Ibsen and Zola. And Woman, always held to be delicate, had succumbed more severely than most. 'Life has taken on a strange unloveliness', wrote Mrs Roy Devereux in 1895, 'and the least beautiful thing therein is the New Woman.'[2]

Violently abused by many, ridiculed by the less hysterical, and championed by a select few, the New Woman became a focal point for a variety of the controversies which rocked the nineties. In the comparatively permissive atmosphere of the time, feminist thinkers were provided with a unique opportunity for a radical investigation of the female role, and ideas ranged adventurously over all aspects of women's life. Highly qualified women were emerging as a result of concessions wrung from the educational establishment and suitable work and social status had to be found for them: the Girton Girl and the Lady Doctor became recognised sub-groups of the New Woman species, and the financial independence and personal fulfilment gained through work began to seem attractive alternatives to marriage. It was pointed out that women were likely to remain the weaker sex as long as they were encased in whalebone and confined their physical activity to the decorous movements of the ballroom, and the new 'doctrine of hygiene' as it was coyly termed advocated sports for women and Rational Dress. Many young women pedalled their way to undreamt-of freedoms on the newly popular bicycle; petticoats and chaperons were equally inappropriate accompaniments, and could be discarded in one go. But these things alone, though important aspects of emancipation, could not account for the elevation of the New Woman into a symbol of all that was most challenging and dangerous in advanced thinking. The crucial factor was, inevitably, sex.

It was suddenly discovered that women, who had for so long been assiduously protected from reading about sex in novels and periodicals, or from hearing about it in polite conversation, had a great deal to say on the subject themselves. Unsavoury topics which had previously lurked in pamphlets, government reports and weighty medical tomes were dragged out by reforming women and paraded triumphantly through the pages of magazines and popular novels. Venereal disease, contraception, divorce and adultery were made the common talking points of the new womanhood. And marriage, traditionally regarded as woman's ultimate goal and highest reward, came in for a tremendous battery of criticism. Mild reformers, like Sarah Grand, deplored the constricting divorce laws and the condition of carefully nurtured ignorance and total inexperience in which young girls were supposed to choose their life partners; but radicals, such as Mona Caird, regarded the whole institution of marriage with such disfavour as to positively recommend its abolition. Some women jeered openly at the ideal of the maternal instinct, and scorned the notion that the care of children was the highest duty to which they should aspire. The family, long regarded as a microcosm of the state, if not of the divine order, was exposed as a nest of seething frustrations, discontent and deception. It was little wonder that, with such wild notions in her head, the New Woman was regarded with some dismay.

Feminist thinkers in the late eighties and nineties appeared to be redirecting their energies from specific political and legal questions towards the formulation of a new morality, a new code of behaviour and sexual ethics. A complete reassessment of the female character was called for, sweeping aside the old clichés and moral certitudes and replacing them with a questioning frankness which alarmed as much as it excited. And here, of course, the novel could play a significant role. A new frankness, particularly about women, was just what was needed to give the English novel the injection of vitality and reality it so badly required. It was not simply male domination and entrenched attitudes which impeded the development of feminist ideas. The unofficial censorship exercised by the circulating libraries, whose refusal to take a book could spell financial disaster for the author, by magazine editors wary of serialising a novel which might offend their readers, and indeed by public opinion, meant that for most of the nineteenth century a novelist would have little chance of publishing a work which seriously challenged accepted standards of delicacy. But by the last decade of the century novelists who were sensitive to the ideas of the feminist debate or who were anxious to develop artistically a fresh view of women and sexual relationships could command an increasingly wide and eager audience. Major novelists, such as Hardy, Meredith and Gissing, joined the battle for artistic freedom and began to write explicitly about topics associated with the New Woman; and in the 1890s a group of popular writers dubbed 'the New Woman novelists' created a sensation with their highly polemical, and often lurid, feminist fiction. Heroines who refused to conform to the traditional feminine role, challenged accepted ideals of marriage and maternity, chose to work for a living, or who in any way argued the feminist cause, became commonplace in the works of both major and minor writers and were firmly identified by readers and reviewers as New Women. How far this assumption was just – what, in detail, it meant – are questions to be examined later. The important point is that for this brief period at least the emancipation of women and the emancipation of the English novel advanced together.

This apparent revolution could not grow out of nothing: the New Woman, while attracting all the notoriety of sensationalism, was in many ways a natural development of the more modest 'advanced' or 'modern' women who, in company with sympathetic men, had been pressing for reforms throughout the century. The 'woman question' had formed an essential part of Victorian thought during most of the reign, and there had already been much agonising over both the formal status of women and general conceptions of the female role. To some extent the two are linked – there is no point in agitating for a woman's right to become a doctor while an accepted definition of feminity is a shrinking from the physical facts of life – but for the convenience of brief summaries they can be considered separately.

Although the official concessions made to women in the nineteenth century look paltry by modern standards they did mark essential steps in the struggle for emancipation. By the 1880s the prospects for the woman who was not going to confine herself to the smooth career of wife and mother were significantly less bleak than at the beginning of the century. The educational establishment, though fighting a strenuous rearguard action, was giving ground on several fronts. The foundation of Queen's and Bedford Colleges in London in 1848 and 1849 paved the way to higher education and produced the first generation of well-qualified women teachers. The North London Collegiate in 1850 and Cheltenham Ladies' College in 1854 set a high standard of secondary education; and the great triumph of 1869, the foundation of Girton, gave women their first foot in the door for the assault on Oxford and Cambridge. Largely owing to the individual efforts of such women as Elizabeth Blackwell, Elizabeth Garrett and Sophia Jex-Blake, the medical profession began with extreme reluctance to relent towards women. Areas of female employment expanded as nurses and teachers began to receive professional training. And the commercial world provided an entirely new field of work: the census returns of 1861 and 1871 show no female clerks at all; by 1881 there were nearly 6000 and by 1891 the number had almost trebled to 17,859 – the Typewriter Girl had arrived.

The legal picture was perhaps not quite so encouraging. Though the Matrimonial Causes Act of 1857 meant that divorce was no longer a total impossibility for the majority, it embodied in law a tacitly accepted moral inequality which proved very hard to dislodge. In effect it gave legal recognition to the common assumption that women should be sexually purer than men. Whereas a husband could sue for divorce simply on the grounds of his wife's adultery, a wife could petition only if her husband had been guilty of 'incestuous adultery, or of rape, or of sodomy or bestiality, or of adultery coupled with such cruelty as without adultery would have entitled her to a divorce *a mensa et thoro*, or of adultery coupled with desertion without reasonable excuse, for two years and upwards'.[3] Thanks to the efforts of Caroline Norton, the Infants' Custody Act was passed in 1839, granting non-adulterous wives the privilege of retaining the children of a broken marriage, provided they were under seven years old. The Married Woman's Property Act of 1882 gave women a legal right to their own property after marriage, a right which suggested to some that a powerful incentive for discontented wives to remain married had been irresponsibly removed. But the vote was apparently no nearer. In 1870 the Suffrage Bill was definitely blocked, and the death of John Stuart Mill in 1873 dealt a crippling blow to the hopes of campaigners. Not until 1895, when the new parliament was returned with more than half the members theoretically committed to the principle of women's suffrage, were hopes revived, though in the event these again proved vain.

However, it was not really until the militant suffragette movement of the early twentieth century that the vote began to be regarded as the cure for all female oppression. Towards the end of the nineteenth century the emphasis fell on questions of social organisation, and particularly of sexual morality, and here again the New Woman was building on earlier foundations. One of the most interesting of mid-century writers on sexual matters was George Drysdale, whose book *The Elements of Social Science or Physical, Sexual and Natural Religion* was first published in 1854 and quickly ran through several editions. Drysdale deplores 'the morbid delicacy, which forbids all open discussion of sexual matters', and sets about remedying the situation in several hundred pages of close print which combine tedium, quirkiness and good sense in more or less equal proportions. His comments on marriage could have come from the mouth of any New Woman of the nineties: 'Marriage is one of the chief instruments in the degradation of women. It perpetuates the old inveterate error, that it is the province of the female sex to depend upon man for support, and to attend merely to household cares and the rearing of children.'[4] But his objections to marriage are not based solely on an altruistic concern for female emancipation; there are medical questions involved too. It was Drysdale's belief that certain diseases could be cured only by sexual intercourse. Obviously this was a difficult prescription to issue if marriage was a necessary preliminary to the implementation of the cure, so freer sexual relations were not only socially, but medically, desirable. It was doubtful, though, that the mothers of ailing young ladies would flock to Dr Drysdale for advice. More practically, he devoted a large section of the book to advocating contraception and describing the most reliable methods then available. Poverty, he argues, is the greatest of social evils, and its 'only cause' is overpopulation. Fortunately there exists a corresponding 'only cure', but before describing it Drysdale goes heavily on the defensive, earnestly exhorting the reader 'not to prejudge this greatest of questions, not to allow commonly received opinions to divert him from its steadfast consideration'. With infinite caution, he leads up to the shocking truth: 'there is a way' which 'contains within itself little real evil, or at least the smallest possible amount of evil'; and at last, no doubt to the relief of what must by now be a very jittery reader, he springs it – 'PREVENTIVE SEXUAL INTER-COURSE'. The ensuing description of such methods as the safe period, the sheath, the sponge (highly recommended) and withdrawal is, however, fairly straightforward, and could no doubt prove of immense benefit to any overburdened wives who had had the courage to follow him to his conclusion.

Drysdale was also indirectly involved in the Bradlaugh–Besant case, which in 1877 gave the contraception question the greatest publicity it had yet received. Charles Bradlaugh and Annie Besant decided to republish *The Fruits of Philosophy* more as a challenge to the Obscene Publications Act than as an advertisement for birth control, but inevitably it was contraception, rather than the freedom of the press, which commanded attention. *The Fruits of Philosophy* by Charles Knowlton, first published in Britain in 1834, described various methods of contraception and had sold steadily but in modest numbers ever since its appearance. When its latest publisher, Charles Watts, also a sub-editor on Bradlaugh's *National Reformer*, was prosecuted under the Obscene Publications Act and pleaded guilty, Bradlaugh and Besant hastened to re-establish the cause of freethinking by provoking another trial. They reissued *The Fruits of Philosophy* with notes by George Drysdale and sold vast numbers of it before the law finally rose to the bait and arrested them. The outcome of the trial and subsequent appeal was acquittal on a technicality, but the almost inadvertent significance of the case was the enormous amount of publicity given to contraception in the national press. It became increasingly difficult for even the most determinedly modest to pretend ignorance of the question, and *The Fruits of Philosophy*, together with Annie Besant's updated account of contraception *The Law of Population*, enjoyed enormous sales. By the end of the century the practice of birth control had become fairly widespread among the middle classes, and was firmly attached to the feminist cause.

General discussions of sexual questions and the increase of knowledge about contraception were obviously important steps in the build up towards the radical feminist thinking of the eighties and nineties. But by far the best and most powerful plea for female emancipation before the emergence of the New Woman came in John Stuart Mill's *The Subjection of Women* (1869). Though many of his points had been made earlier by Mary Wollstonecraft in *A Vindication of the Rights of Women* (1792), she had been so far ahead of her time as to be practically lost sight of, and it was Mill's work which became the bible of the feminists in the latter part of the nineteenth century. Mill's case for 'a principle of perfect equality' is argued with incisive logic and meticulously covers the ground from equality before the law, in government, the professions and education down to equality of influence in domestic matters and power-sharing in marriage. Probably his major achievement, though, was to spell out with greater clarity than any previous writer the psychological pressures which kept women in their traditional place: in modern terminology, he spotted the indoctrination of sex-roles. 'All women', he writes,

> are brought up from the very earliest years in the belief that their ideal of character is the very opposite to that of men; not self-will, and government by self-control, but submission, and yielding to the control of others. All the moralities tell them that it is the duty of women, and all the current sentimentalities that it is their nature, to live for others; to make complete abnegation of themselves, and to have no life but in their affections.[5]

This leads on to an attack on the notion of 'natural' feminity, always one of the prime weapons of the anti-feminist. Mill effectively demolishes the idea that what is instinctively apprehended as 'natural' must be so, and more particularly that anybody can pronounce with certainty on what is naturally feminine. Women, he says, have always hitherto been kept, as far as regards spontaneous development, in so unnatural a state, that their nature cannot but have been greatly distorted and disguised; and no one can safely pronounce that if women's nature was left to choose its direction as freely as men's, and if no artificial bent were attempted to be given to it except that required by the conditions of human society, and given to both sexes alike, there would be any material difference, or perhaps any difference at all, in the character and capacities which would unfold themselves.[6]

This was an exciting idea: if women could only set aside the assumptions about their own nature ground into them from earliest infancy and forge ahead towards any goal they may choose, there was no limit to their possible achievements. Deviation from the accepted pattern of feminine behaviour need no longer be regarded as 'unnatural' – it could just as well be called 'spontaneous development'.

There were powerful indications even before the publication of Mill's essay that many women were choosing to develop spontaneously, and were attracting a good deal of adverse comment as a result. A general feeling that young ladies were not what they used to be was already creating nervous flutters in the conventionally-minded, and this feeling was skilfully exploited by one of the most ardent anti-feminists of the period, Mrs Lynn Linton. In 1868 the *Saturday Review* published what was to become one of its most famous articles, 'The Girl of the Period',[7] which created intense controversy and whose title passed into the language. Mrs Lynn Linton's portrayal of modern womanhood was certainly not calculated to allay fears, but at least appeared to identify an enemy. Nostalgically she summons up a picture of the 'fair young English girl' of the past, a paragon 'who, when she married, would be her husband's friend and companion, but never his rival . . . a tender mother, an industrious housekeeper, a judicious mistress'. The contrast with the present is acutely painful, for the modern young woman apparently has more in common with the prostitute than with the angel in the house: 'The girl of the period is a creature who dyes her hair and paints her face'; her inordinate regard for fashion leads her to 'strong, bold talk and freshness; to the love of pleasure and indifference to duty; to the desire of money before either love or happiness; to uselessness at home, dissatisfaction with the monotony of ordinary life, and horror of all useful work'. She apes the manner of the *demi-mondaine* with the result that 'men are afraid of her; and with reason'. Mrs Lynn Linton concludes, sweepingly but with tremendous popular appeal:

> All men whose opinion is worth having prefer the simple and genuine girl of the past, with her tender little ways and pretty, bashful modesties, to this loud and rampant modernisation, with her false red hair and painted skin, talking slang as glibly as a man, and by preference leading the conversation to doubtful subjects.

It might appear that this fast and unalluring creature could have little to do with the deep sincerity of the reforming modern woman. The predatory manhunter with her painted face and dyed hair seems very far indeed from the New Woman's ideals of integrity and independence. But the traditionalist public was in no mood to discriminate, and the Girl of the Period image was superimposed on any picture of modern womanhood. In any case, some of Mrs Lynn Linton's pronouncements, though much inflated and distorted for rhetorical effect, could be identified with feminist ideas. 'Strong, bold talk and freshness', for example, could be interpreted as a laudable reluctance to draw on the reserves of false modesty supposed to be at the command of every girl. 'Dissatisfaction with the monotony of ordinary life' was surely not so heinous a crime that it should imply exclusion from the ranks of decent society, and Mrs Lynn Linton's ideal of English womanhood – 'tender, loving, retiring or domestic' – could not be expected to appeal to the new spirit of adventure. Indeed it was this very image, held up by so many for imitation by the ideal Englishwoman, that was being so vigorously challenged. Sarah Ellis's best-selling books of the 1840s, which codified at length proper feminine behaviour, retained their popular following, and there were still battalions of Lynn Lintons who would endorse her rhetoric:

> Can it be a subject of regret to any kind and feeling woman, that her sphere of action is one adapted to the exercise of the affections, where she may love, and trust, and hope, and serve, to the utmost of her wishes? Can it be a subject of regret that she is not called upon, so much as man, to calculate, to compete, to struggle, but rather occupy a sphere in which the elements of discord cannot

with propriety be admitted – in which beauty and order are expected to denote her presence, and where the exercise of benevolence is the duty she is most frequently called upon to perform?[8]

The New Woman's answer to these questions would be an emphatic and defiant Yes.

By the 1890s, then, when the New Woman began to emerge with a distinct identity, a good deal of progress had been achieved in the two areas most affecting modern woman. Reforms in the law and in educational and professional institutions had opened up a wider range of opportunities than had ever previously been available; and frank discussions of sexual questions, together with rational investigations of woman's place in contemporary society, had done much to dispel the stifling clouds of mystique which had gathered protectively round the fair sex.

The New Woman built on both foundations. She could now elect to put her energies into professional rather than matrimonial achievement, and could justify her decision by pointing out that marriage, as conventionally defined, was a state little better than slavery. She could make her own choice about having children, either with or without the authority of a marriage licence, and she could demand complete freedom from either parental or legal control in selecting her sexual partner. In fact, the New Woman represented everything that was daring and revolutionary, everything that was challenging to the norms of female behaviour dictated by the Lynn Lintons and Sarah Ellises. But two essential points have to be borne in mind if an accurate picture of the New Woman is to emerge. Firstly, a woman was only genuinely New if her conflict with social convention was on *a matter of principle*. Mere eccentricity, or flamboyance along the Girl of the Period lines were not sufficient. The New Woman had high ideals; she examined the world from an intelligent and informed base, and if what she saw led her to the conclusion that accepted standards were unjust or inadequate then she would try to go her own way according to her own principles. Secondly, the New Woman's radical stance was taken on matters of personal choice. It was not based on any recognisable movement or organisation, and was necessarily limited to the areas where personal choice could operate. A woman at the end of the nineteenth century could not choose to vote in a general election, but she could opt for bachelor motherhood, or a career, or even, on a trivial level, short hair, comfortable clothes and a cigarette. Any one of these, provided it was accompanied by stern pronouncements on its liberating effect, would be enough to label its perpetrator a New Woman. And in many ways this attack on domestic and social arrangements, even though unaccompanied by violent demonstrations, incendiarism and suicide, was a good deal more dramatic, and more significant in terms of total female emancipation, than the suffrage struggle which eventually superseded it.

Intelligent, individualistic and principled, the New Woman was also essentially middle-class. Working-class women, while no longer hauling coal in mines eleven hours a day, still led lives so totally remote from the cosy domesticity and shining feminine ideal against which the New Woman was reacting that this kind of revolt could do nothing for them. It was pointless to warn a working-class woman against the evils of an arranged marriage to a dissolute aristocrat, or to urge her to undertake activities more fulfilling than embroidery and visiting. The problems of working-class women were entirely different from those of the middle classes, and received very little attention from writers on the New Woman.

We have, then, some sort of composite picture of the New Woman. More precise definitions are bound to be elusive, since the lack of any formal organisation meant that the principles on which she acted would be largely dictated by individual circumstance or interest. But as many people regarded the New Woman as no more than a malicious invention of journalists, it is worth looking at the treatment she got from the press. This after all is largely what created the public image, and set the context in which the novels dealing with the new type of heroine were judged. There can be no doubt that the New Woman provided the popular press with an endless source of amusement. Cartoonists, naturally enough, seized on externals, and portrayed her in academic dress, or with short hair and mannish clothes, and even, in one *Punch* cartoon, with a gun under her arm (the caption implies that, though bloodthirsty, the New Woman is a poor shot). It is also clear that even if comfortingly non-existent, she could still be severely damaging to the more restrained feminists. Elizabeth Chapman was one writer who scented the danger from the 'impatient and ill-balanced minds' of New Women to the more respectable feminist aims:

I believe that these have been obscured to a rather serious extent of late by the interminable flood of gaseous chatter to which the invention of a journalistic myth known as the 'New Woman' has given rise, and that it has become necessary sharply to emphasise the distinction between this phantom and the real reformer and friend of her sex and of humanity whom I would call the 'Best Woman'.[9]

Another typical response was amused tolerance. Richard le Gallienne, in an article on 'The New Womanhood',[10] relates what he obviously feels to be the charming tale of his encounter with one of its representatives. She is 'a dear, brown-eyed child of nineteen', who is regrettably forced to go out into the world to earn a living. He lures her into an apparently sensible discussion of qualifications, salary and promotion prospects, but all the while his thoughts are elsewhere: 'It amused me that the possibility of these calculations being rendered superfluous by a happy marriage never seemed to occur to her'. His eyes begin to wander too: 'her maidenhood was of that warm-eyed full-bosomed type that as plainly prophesies motherhood as the blossom half transformed into fruit prophesies autumn'. When he puts these points to her, her understandable disgust merely gives him opportunity for more twinkling-eyed condescension: 'You should have seen her draw herself up and protest her scorn of any such base compromise'. Exactly the response, in fact, to make the New Woman with the gun take speedy steps to improve her aim.

A more serious analysis of the New Woman's principles was given in a series of six articles run by the *Saturday Review* in 1895.[11] Snappily titled 'Dies Dominae, by a Woman of the Day' these essays were designed to promote sympathy with the New Woman and to give a reasoned defence of her ideas. Lest this should be too readily achieved, however, a right of rejoinder was granted to 'Lady Jeune' who stepped in smartly at the conclusion of the three most controversial articles to deliver a blow on behalf of the Old woman. We therefore have an interesting confrontation between the new and the old in a context of reasonably temperate debate, and the attitudes taken by each side are clearly and neatly contrasted.

The article on 'The Maternal Instinct' is particularly revealing, since it is accepted by both sides that families are decreasing in size – presumably as a result of more widespread contraception – and that there is a marked reluctance among married women to devote the best years of their lives exclusively to the rearing of children. Where they differ, of course, is on the reasons for this and its desirability. The Woman of the Day puts her case with vigour, contemptuously dismissing the maternal ideal: 'The only woman at the present time who is willing to be regarded as a mere breeding machine is she who lacks the wit to adopt any other *rôle*'. She argues that the New Woman, by examining the question of motherhood rationally and without prejudice, has exposed the immorality of indiscriminate breeding – women physically wrecked by the age of thirty, children born into families unable to give them proper care – and has demonstrated the practical superiority of intelligence over instinctive or 'natural' femininity. The New Woman 'has seen enough to make her recoil with horror from the heedless motherhood which was accounted the glory of the instinctive woman. Such maternity may be natural, but it is scarcely civilised, and to call it divine is sheer cant'. The only good mother, she suggests, is one prepared to limit her breeding capacity, one who has more to offer her child than an endless succession of siblings and a vapid ideal of maternal devotion. 'After centuries of motherhood, woman at large is beginning to be simply – woman.'

On the contrary, retorts Lady Jeune, 'woman, as the mother, represents the most sacred idea in life'. 'No woman', she declares uncompromisingly, 'knows what real joy is till her babe is laid in her arms.' This is good conventional stuff, of course, and no doubt comforting to those readers who had just seen themselves stigmatised as mere witless breeding machines. Lady Jeune concedes, though, that especially among the middle classes 'the size of the family is diminishing rapidly'. But she attributes this not to the sense of responsibility and desire for self-fulfilment seen as the mark of the New Woman, but to a frivolous craving for social pleasures closer to Mrs Lynn Linton's conception of the Girl of the Period: 'The real fact is, that women do not have children because it is irksome and interferes with their amusements'. On the question of children the new and old are irreconcilably divided.

As might be expected, this is also the case with the discussion on 'The Value of Love'. 'Love' here is obviously a euphemism for sex, and even the champion of the New Woman is forced into an apologetic strain. A certain amount of sympathetic understanding is required, she implies, if the New Woman's overconcentration on 'the physical' is to be excused:

With the awakening of the intellect there has been a coincident awakening of the senses. All through the centuries the physical faculties of woman have either lain dormant or have been exercised instinctively without comprehension. Now, for the first time in her progress towards perfect knowledge, their significance has been revealed to her, and as yet she can think of nothing else.

During the first thrill of emancipation, in other words, excitement over the awakening of 'physical faculties' might overwhelm all other interests; but things will simmer down, gradually returning to a state of calm when 'the desire of the flesh and its satisfaction becomes an inconsiderable incident in life, instead of the aim and end of it'.

Despite the circumlocutions, it is clear that the New Woman is regarded as a highly sexual being, all the more dangerous since she cannot be dismissed as a prostitute or a fallen woman. Lady Jeune produces the obligatory shudder of revulsion and defends the cause of purity with a flat denial: 'I look among the women of England for the shameless and insatiate creature, who, I am told, represents the New Woman of the time, and I cannot find her'. Researches lead her to the reassuring conclusion that 'the average English woman is a cold, almost passionless, creature, to whom the allurements of passion offer small temptation', but she still feels it necessary to issue a prophetic warning: 'The voyage of discovery on which the New Woman is embarking will end on the rocks of a life's shipwreck'.

Even her champion expressed some qualms about the New Woman, particularly deploring her demand for work rather than leisured ease. But these, and even Lady Jeune's stern rejoinders, pale into insignificance when compared with the wrath of Mrs Lynn Linton. She strode into the attack with all her customary zest, and again presented an alarming figure who combined many of the ideals of the New Woman – stated of course in extreme and derogatory terms – with some more eccentric attributes. The Girl of the Period has now matured into a Wild Woman, whose

> ideal of life for herself is absolute personal independence coupled with supreme power over men. She repudiates the doctrine of individual conformity for the sake of general good; holding the self-restraint involved as an act of slavishness of which no woman worth her salt would be guilty. She makes between the sexes no distinctions, moral or aesthetic, nor even personal; but holds that what is lawful to the one is permissible to the other.[12]

Except for the tone, there is little in this to which the New Woman would take exception apart from the 'supreme power over men'. Nor would she object, as Mrs Lynn Linton does, to women who indulge in such unladylike activities as tennis or golf or earning a living. But when Mrs Lynn Linton really gets into her stride she produces an extraordinary picture of a powder-encrusted harridan lounging around with the men after dinner, smoking, drinking, gambling and in her spare time – for some obscure reason – breeding horses.

After reading Mrs Lynn Linton one might be excused for approaching the question of the New Woman's actual existence with some trepidation. But while it is difficult to produce instances of female horse-breeders gazing blearily through their make-up at a roulette wheel, there is independent corroboration from women of the time that a more responsibly revolutionary life-style was becoming increasingly possible. Many of the writers who won fame with New Woman novels were prepared to put their theories into practice. Ménie Muriel Dowie explored the Carpathian mountains entirely alone, dressed in tight trousers and thigh boots; 'George Egerton' (Mary Chavelita Dunne) earned her own living in three continents, married twice and took lovers; Olive Schreiner travelled widely in England, Europe and South Africa, wrote highly respected political works and was an intimate friend of Havelock Ellis. But there had always been individual women who refused to conform. We gain a more convincing picture of strong minority protest from the pages of an extraordinary magazine, the *Adult*, whose stormy career lasted from June 1897 to March 1899. The *Adult* was essentially a sex magazine which offered a social conscience in place of pornography. The first editorial declared that 'its pages will be open for the discussion of important phases of sex questions which are almost universally ignored elsewhere' and promised sympathy with the New Woman's ideal of personal freedom in determining moral codes:

> The name of our paper, the Adult, signifies that we recognise the paramount right of the individual to self-realisation in all non-invasive directions. The Adult advocates the absolute freedom of two individuals of full age, to enter into and conclude at will, any mutual relationships whatever, where no third person's material interests are concerned.[13]

The *Adult* presents us with a remarkable picture of sexual liberation in the late nineteenth century. Its discussions of homosexuality and lesbianism are frank and tolerant without being remotely prurient; the ringing calls for Free Love which echo through almost every number are often accompanied by case histories of couples who can speak for its efficacy as a cure for all social ills; and its radical feminist stance often produces ideas for sexual equality far in advance of more mainstream – and perhaps more practical – women's movements. Though passionately advocating contraception as the greatest of all boons to the emancipated woman, it conceded that the total extinction of the human race was not a desirable end of the feminist campaign, and devoted a good deal of space to attempts to reconcile the ideal of freedom for women with the necessity for a certain amount of breeding. A government-sponsored child benefit scheme was one proposal, and another, which has only just crept back into modern feminist manifestos, was a fair wage for housewives. The *Adult*'s tone is crusading and hopeful, and based throughout on the assumption that many people are already leading lives of exemplary liberation. 'There are women', declared Lillian Harman, 'brave, true *womanly* women, too – who live their lives in freedom, calmly ignoring conventional commands.' And in a later number the same writer gave a glowing account of the New Woman:

> Nature does not force the 'new woman' to assume a position inferior to her lover, in any relation of life. She will sustain only the relations which she herself desires, will be happy in the love of her lover, and tenacious of her own self-respect; and her children will imbibe the spirit of their free mother, and will be happy, healthy, and independent – in marked contrast to the offspring of the 'submitting' slave mother.[14]

Undoubtedly there were women whose mode of life could identify them as New, and the wide and often hysterical press coverage had created an impression of large-scale revolt. But for the vast majority, ideas greatly outstripped practice. The New Woman was held up as a symbolic figurehead for a type of social rebellion which many women might concede to be generally desirable but personally unattainable; yet since the New Woman rebelled essentially against personal circumstances, the most effective way of portraying her was not in journalistic summaries of her principles, but in novels. It was the novel which could investigate in detail the

clash between radical principles and the actualities of contemporary life, which could portray most convincingly the stifling
social conventions from which the New Woman was trying to break
free, and which could present arguments for new standards of
morality, new codes of behaviour, in the context of an easily
recognisable social world. The conventional concerns of the
popular novel – love, marriage, the family – were the conventional
concerns of women, and a fictional heroine who took a fresh look at
these would provide a more obvious point of identification for a
sheltered middle-class reader than the alarming and sometimes
monstrous New Woman figures created by the press. And novelists
stood to gain too. For the New Woman the destruction of sexual
taboos appeared essential to female emancipation; and if there was
one thing Victorian fiction needed above all else it was the removal
of what Hardy called the 'insuperable bar' which prevented the
inclusion in a novel of any overt treatment of sex. The portrayal of a
new type of heroine would almost inevitably entail a franker
approach to sexuality, and would open vast new areas of female
psychology and behaviour which had previously been excluded
from the novelist's range.

Few novelists specifically identified their heroines as New
Women – the term was too loaded with associations of eccentricity
and fanaticism – but a great many novels which appeared in the
nineties seemed to contemporary readers to be directly propagating
the New Woman's ideas. Marriage, which had usually provided the
conventional happy ending, began to be used more frequently as a
beginning, and a bad one at that. By minutely dissecting unfortunate marriages, novelists showed ordinary women arriving
through bitter experience at the New Woman's principle of
personal freedom in selecting sexual partners. Meredith's *Lord
Ormont and his Aminta*, Gissing's *The Odd Women* and Hardy's *Jude
the Obscure* were all widely interpreted as problem novels on the New
Woman theme. Alternatives to marriage, including divorce and
free love, were enthusiastically canvassed in fiction, and Grant
Allen's enormously popular *The Woman Who Did* became the
archetypal anti-marriage novel. Female sexuality was made
fashionable by George Egerton, who received hundreds of effusive
letters from women grateful for seeing their unmentionable feelings
given the seal of respectability in print. Motherhood was ruthlessly
stripped of its sentimental trappings, and some novelists imitated
Ibsen and showed their heroines slamming the door on husband and

children. The ideal of female purity was investigated: should it, as the traditionalists maintained, consist in carefully nurtured ignorance of the harsher facts of life, or should it rather be based on knowledge and understanding – even experience? When Hardy sub-titled *Tess of the D'Urbervilles* 'A Pure Woman' he was – as he must have known perfectly well – issuing a deliberately provocative challenge to conventional notions of purity. Altogether the period is rich in novels which show women being led through the normal incidents of domestic life to a point where circumstances compel them to discard their old assumptions and strike out into a more radical course of thought or action.

Obviously this break through the conventional bounds of fiction carried far-reaching implications for the freedom of the novel in general and the portrayal of women in particular. When a respected novelist like Hardy was savagely berated in the press for the alleged obscenity of *Jude the Obscure*, more enlightened critics were impelled to dispute the desirability of artistic restraint and initiate important debates on the freedom of fiction. Woman writers who used the novel as a propaganda machine for feminist ideas, and who presented heroines indulging in minutely detailed self-analysis, encouraged others to reassess the fictional portrayal of the female character. 'It is only lately that woman has really begun to turn herself inside out, as it were, and to put herself into her books', wrote Hugh Stutfield in an article on 'The Psychology of Feminism'. 'Man has no idea what it feels like to be a woman, but it will not be her fault if he does not soon begin in some degree to understand.'[15] But the social implications were also grave. It was generally feared that what women read about, they might do, and thus the new type of novel appeared to threaten the whole domestic structure. Torrents of abuse were poured on the writers of New Woman novels. They were 'petticoat anarchists who put a blazing torch to the shrine of self-respect and feminine shame',[16] 'women who appear to have cultivated the intellect at the expense of all womanly feeling and instinctive delicacy, and to have cast aside all reticence in the mad desire to make others eat as freely as themselves of the forbidden fruit of the tree of knowledge'.[17] The general conclusion was that 'if the New Woman elects to be judged by the fiction she writes, reads, and applauds, nay – may we not justly add – inspires, then she must . . . accept the position of the bitterest foe to the cherished modesty of our sex that the century has known'.[18]

Thus the emergence of the New Woman as a social phenomenon

was matched by an increasing interest among novelists in the woman question as a source of artistic inspiration. Minor writers in particular, content for the most part to parade their arguments unencumbered with the literary trappings of imaginative power or psychological plausibility, gave stark and forceful expression to the new feminist ideas. And the themes they tackled were integrated with greater skill into the works of more talented novelists. Where these works differed from the mainstream of earlier Victorian fiction was in the extent to which they were prepared to provoke a clash with accepted social convention which would reverberate outside the world of the novel. In portraying marital breakdown, adultery, free love or bachelor motherhood unaccompanied by the approved moral retribution – or indeed heavily supported by an impassioned moral defence – these novels were ruthlessly hacking away the foundations of idealised femininity on which much of the Victorian moral structure was built. More or less overtly they were broadcasting the ideas of the New Woman, and an avid public hung on their every word, eager to be either loftily inspired or deliciously shocked.

An investigation of the works of minor New Woman novelists – minor only in the sense that they produced nothing of lasting literary merit, since their novels sold in enormous quantities – will give us the clearest picture of the themes treated and the new character types which emerged. It will then become apparent how far major novelists were responding to the radical feminist thinking of the time and to what extent they were influenced by the works of their less talented colleagues. But before turning to the New Woman of popular fiction, it is worth looking at the ways in which the ideas she developed were treated in the earlier Victorian novel. This will give some idea of the degree to which deference to publicly approved morality limited the nineteenth-century novel; it will reveal some of the conventions surrounding the fictional portrayal of women, and provide a useful comparison by which to judge the revolutionary nature of the New Woman novel.

I Marriage, Morality and the Model Woman

Marriage is the mainstay of Victorian fiction. Even in novels where the normal preliminaries of courtship, heartbreak and reconciliation do not form the basis of the plot, a wedding can provide a convenient conclusion. The novel ends, but the characters are directed forwards into an assured future of household concerns, children, domestic harmony. It is a comforting picture, and could be painted innumerable times. That it was not drawn accurately from the life, however, was sufficiently apparent to make many novelists vary the pattern, either by retouching the central figures, as Thackeray does in *Vanity Fair*, or by introducing contrasting tones. Prostitutes hover menacingly or pathetically on the fringes of novels by Dickens, Trollope and Mrs Gaskell. Seduction and betrayal, adultery and shameful pregnancies are accepted plot devices in fiction throughout the period. With such an emphasis on sexual relationships, it may seem remarkable that the Victorian novel maintained its circumspection and moral conformity for so long. In fact, sexual transgressions, unhappy marriages and even acute perceptions about the position of women in society, could be assimilated with reasonable ease into an entirely acceptable moral scheme. All the data of the New Woman novel were present in earlier fiction: it was the interpretation which so radically differed.

In the more robust world of the pre-Victorian novel, sexuality is a normal part of life. If a heroine from this period wishes to remain pure – and some do not – she must be continually on her guard. Fanny Burney shows us a brutal society, in which innocence is continually assaulted: women of the world laugh derisively at the scrupulous morality of the Evelinas and Camillas, and seducers habitually lurk in wait for young girls, post-chaise at the ready. In Jane Austen, the simmering underworld of illicit passions occupied by such characters as Willoughby can easily bubble over into an apparently well-regulated society. Both these writers of course condemn sexual relationships unsanctified by marriage, but neither allows rational perception of immorality to be overlaid with pious amazement that such depravity should exist. Indeed Jane Austen is often humorous at the expense of those whose dismay at others' misdemeanours becomes disproportionate. Fanny Price, on hearing of Maria's affair with Henry Crawford, whips herself into such an orgy of outrage that finally 'it appeared to her, that as far as this world alone was concerned, the greatest blessing to everyone of kindred with Mrs Rushworth would be instant annihilation'. Two paragraphs later, when she learns that the crisis has recalled her to Mansfield Park, 'she was . . . in the greatest danger of being exquisitely happy'. Similarly, in *Pride and Prejudice* the very real distress caused by Lydia's elopement with Wickham is comically qualified by the banality of Mary's 'moral extractions from the evil before them' and the sententious sermonising of Mr Collins.

In the mid-nineteenth-century novel sexual misdemeanours are more usually treated as hideous aberrations and are approached with uniform gravity and a stern moral frown. The fallen woman was a stain on society and had to be punished, either by the intolerable pangs of conscience or by death – preferably both. Even the novelist who took the rather advanced line that many such women were victims, that they did not jump but were pushed to their fall by some callous profligate, could not dispense with final retribution. The idea expressed later by some of the New Woman novelists, and by Hardy and Meredith, that women conventionally 'fallen' might actually have chosen their state on moral grounds would have appeared utterly incomprehensible. Mary Bennet's 'useful lesson' drawn from her sister's disgrace – 'that loss of female virtue is irretrievable – that one false step involves her in endless ruin – that her reputation is no less brittle than it is beautiful' – was known by heart, and faithfully trotted out, though at far greater length, in many novels.

One of the most notable of these was Mrs Henry Wood's *East Lynne*, first published in 1861. Melodramatic, sentimental and crudely moralistic, it became a bestseller, starkly illuminating the popular attitude towards erring wives. Its heroine, Lady Isabel Vane, possesses 'a face of surpassing beauty' but no money and, after her father's death, no home. The kindly Mr Carlyle purchases her family house, East Lynne, and proposes to her, but she has conceived a girlish passion for the villainous Frank Levison. His crass confession that he has no intention of marrying her, and avowed desire 'to play the butterfly' give her some inkling that 'he was false and heartless' (an impression already subtly conveyed to the reader when he tramples on a gold cross given to Lady Isabel by her dying mother) so she accepts Carlyle. Unfortunate circumstances, such as the presence at East Lynne of Carlyle's meddlesome and domineering sister, and his habit of keeping midnight assignations with a girl known to be in love with him, make Lady Isabel suspect that she is not loved and valued. She runs off with Levison, bears him a child, is deserted, reported killed in a train crash (which in fact only cripples and disfigures her) and returns in disguise to East Lynne as governess to her own children. Her punishments are severe, and are piled up with sadistic relish: apart from the discomfort she suffers from her mangling in the accident, she has to endure the presence of Carlyle's second wife, and to preside at the deathbed of her own son, the child who, in the dramatised version, so memorably died without addressing her as mother. After revealing her identity, and obtaining a qualified forgiveness from Carlyle, she too expires, with the observation that since there is no marriage in heaven her sin will be forgiven.

Even in outline, it is a curious tale. And the elaborate sub-plot, in which it emerges that Carlyle's nocturnal strolls with his old flame are taken merely to discuss the position of her brother who is accused of a murder actually committed – as we finally learn – by Levison, ensures that the drama is unrelenting. It is a novel which batters the reader with clichés: when characters are surprised they start wildly, when upset they turn deathly pale and are ready to sink to the ground, when undeceived the scales fall from their eyes. Its moral attitudes, ruthlessly hammered home, have the same synthetic but instantly acceptable appeal to popular taste. Lady Isabel is, as we are constantly reminded, an aristocrat, and her conscience is therefore more finely tuned than that of the masses. Hence her initial love for Levison, which fills her with 'terror', has nothing 'vulgar' in it; she believes it impossible 'ever to forsake her duty as a wife, a gentlewoman and a Christian'. But as Peter Coveney points out,[1] the order of priorities in this novel is revealing: Lady Isabel thinks first of her marital status, second of her social position and only last of any fundamental morality. Her crime is primarily social, both in its origin – Levison abuses all the laws of hospitality in wooing Lady Isabel under her husband's roof – and in its repercussions – she brings disgrace and dishonour on her home, leaves her children motherless, and gives birth to a bastard. Only when death looms do characters begin to think in terms of the religion which is meant to uphold their morality, and even then Lady Isabel pictures heaven as a sort of purged and indestructible East Lynne: 'My sin will be remembered no more there, and we shall be together with our children for ever and ever'.

Mrs Henry Wood's overall message is clear and uncompromising – a woman who leaves her husband for another man is lost forever and thoroughly deserves all the punishments that fate and the novelist's ingenuity can devise. She need not expect even fleeting pleasure from her sin. Lady Isabel 'never . . . experienced a moment's calm, or peace, or happiness, since the fatal night of quitting her husband'; from the first she is tormented by the 'adder stings' of conscience, and is accompanied in her exile on the continent by 'a skeleton of living fire, that must prey on her heartstrings forever'. Lest anyone should remain unconvinced, the author turns aside to make a direct exhortation:

> Oh, reader, believe me! Lady – wife – mother! should you ever be tempted to abandon your home . . . whatever trials may be the lot of your married life, though they may magnify themselves to your crushed spirit as beyond the endurance of woman to bear, *resolve* to bear them: fall down upon your knees and pray to be enabled to bear them; pray for patience; pray for strength to resist the demon that would urge you so to escape; bear unto death, rather than forfeit your fair name and your fair conscience; for be assured that the alternative, if you rush on to it, will be found far worse than death. (Vol II, ch. 10)

Better advice might be to check your facts first. Lady Isabel brings disgrace on herself and abandons her home and adored children primarily because she sees her husband in the company of another woman and leaps to the wrong conclusion. And while maxims for good conduct are being dished out, it would seem on the evidence before us that the gentleman-husband-father could do with some too. Carlyle might be told that it is unkind to bring his bride to a home run by his ill-tempered and interfering sister; that it is unwise to invite a patent philanderer like Levison to stay in his house; and above all that some explanation is required when he slinks out at night to meet female friends. In fact, though, the novel is resolutely one-sided in its sympathies. Lady Isabel is bundled off to her doom with the minimum of justification, and Carlyle immediately assumes the role of wronged and noble innocent. He plays the part with aplomb. His first action on hearing of his wife's departure is to announce, with a straight face, that she has gone to a fate worse than death; his next is to order the servants not to address his daughter by her first name, Isabel, and to substitute her second.

Beneath the simple point that adultery is a bad thing lie some interesting moral assumptions. Firstly, the marriage institution must be inviolate; '*whatever* trials' the woman has to bear – even if Lady Isabel had been right in her suspicions of her husband – she must resolve to endure them meekly. That her 'fair name' would be sacrificed if she sought happiness with another man was an unfortunate social fact; but that her equally fair conscience should go the same way would only make sense if it were upheld by a strict and convinced allegiance to the words of the Christian marriage service, a point which the author never troubles to make. Clearly the ideas about marriage expressed here are conceived to fit in with the current principles of social behaviour, and these principles are often glaringly inconsistent. Marriage is serious, even sacred, and is based on love, trust and duty – but it is also a legitimate device for saving face. Lord Mount Severn, Isabel's nearest relative, re-cognises Levison as 'a base, heartless, bad man' but is dismayed that she is not married to him. When he learns that Levison has refused to make an honest woman of her, despite fathering her child, his imprecations are dreadful: 'Coward! sneak! May good men shun him from henceforth! may his Queen refuse to receive him!' In fact Levison finds himself a respectable wife, and though we learn nothing of the sovereign's reaction, her subjects for the most part appear content.

Secondly, there is considerable confusion about the extent to which Lady Isabel should be held responsible for her actions. We are told, for example, that her feeling for Levison 'was not a voluntary one; she could no more repress it than she could repress her own sense of being'. And before agreeing to marry Carlyle she admits frankly that she does not love him, a confession which disturbs him not in the least. Her relatives promote the match because they want her out of the house, and Carlyle shamelessly bribes her into acceptance with the bait of her beloved East Lynne. The implication is that although Isabel cannot help loving Levison, it is a crime that she should do so, and that although she does not love her husband she displays gross ingratitude in not responding adequately to his adoration. Whenever a convincing explanation for her conduct is offered its validity is promptly denied, so that we have a curious muddle of mitigating circumstances which ultimately turn out to have no force. The novel shows that there are a good many excuses for Lady Isabel's behaviour, and continually insists that such behaviour can never be excused.

Mrs Henry Wood's case may be clumsily pasted together, the cracks all too obvious to the modern eye, but because its basic premise was so widely accepted contemporary readers could happily gloss over the rest. Better novelists might not reveal such flagrant inconsistencies but could still exploit the feelings of horror and pathos evoked by the fallen woman without seriously questioning the moral basis for such a response. Dickens's portrayal of Lady Dedlock in *Bleak House* is a striking example. Although she has excellent grounds for believing both her lover and child to be safely dead the mere fact of her having sinned in this way is enough to freeze her into a pose of fashionable boredom for the rest of her life. Even before the detective-story element of the plot begins to unravel the strands of her secret, Dickens intimates that Lady Dedlock is oppressed by a serious sense of guilt: 'Weariness of soul lies before her, as it lies behind – her Ariel has put a girdle of it round the whole earth, and it cannot be unclasped'. So far as she is aware, no innocent party can have suffered – there is no distraught husband, no motherless child; the guilt at this stage is for the act itself.

The loss of female virtue is truly irretrievable, even without Mr Tulkinghorn as a politely detached Nemesis to bring about the endless ruin. It is also apparently contagious. Fallen women who retain any trace of moral virtue are always reluctant to come into contact with innocent young girls. In the scene where Lady Dedlock dramatically announces her relationship to Esther Summerson ('O my child, my child, I am your wicked and unhappy mother!') maternal devotion momentarily overcomes her sense of corruption; but when she remembers what a 'wretched and dishonouring creature' she is, Esther notes that 'she shrank down in my embrace as if she were unwilling that I should touch her'. Similarly what at first appears to be her blameless affection for the servant Rosa turns out after the discovery of her secret to be something which could blight the girl's life as effectively as a dose of smallpox. Mr Tulkinghorn's thinly disguised account of Lady Dedlock's situation anticipates the shame which would be attached to Rosa if the secret were revealed: 'When Mr Rouncewell's townsman heard of the disclosure, he no more allowed the girl to be patronized and honoured, than he would have suffered her to be trodden underfoot before his eyes'. Lady Dedlock promptly dismisses Rosa – 'I do what I can to spare an innocent girl . . . from the taint of my impending shame' – and by her selfless action brings Tulkinghorn to the point of disclosing her past to Sir Leicester.

It is true that Dickens squeezes a good deal of pathos out of Lady Dedlock's sufferings. But that those sufferings are deserved is never denied by anyone, least of all by the victim herself. It is notable too that in the scenes where we are invited to feel most sympathy for her we are also kept keenly alert to the pain she has inflicted on others. In the midst of her tearful reunion with her daughter, who is busily assuring her of total love and forgiveness, we are nudged into resentment on behalf of the deprived child. Esther slips in one of her innocently stinging observations, reminding us that the mother's voice which is now pleading for compassion is one 'which in my childhood I had never learned to love and recognize, had never been sung to sleep with, had never heard a blessing from, had never had a hope inspired by'. Also, though Lady Dedlock did not kill Tulkinghorn the reader is allowed to believe for some time that she did; and even after the true murderer is identified Dickens expends a whole paragraph of extremely complicated prose in analysing the feelings which could have led her to commit the deed, concluding that the 'wicked relief' she feels at his death is much the same as if she had shot him herself. And Sir Leicester's reaction to the disclosure of his wife's past is particularly interesting. Transformed at a stroke from a pompous old buffer into a sadly dependent wreck of a man his anguish is indeed grievous. Clearly this is the time for his true nobility to emerge, as it does when he struggles pitifully with his paralysis to gasp out 'full forgiveness' for his wife. But this is not quite so generous as it appears. The sequence of events is very carefully orchestrated to leave the minimum possibility of reconciliation between the Dedlocks. Sir Leicester is kept conveniently mute, unable to register any detailed response to the event, until he receives the letter in which Lady Dedlock virtually announces her intention of committing suicide. Only then, when it is a matter of life or death, does Sir Leicester divulge his feelings, because only then can they be appropriately heartrending and safely ineffectual. To forgive Lady Dedlock to her face would make nonsense of the preceding action and in any case would leave the very awkward question of how their relationship would be continued. This sort of sin can only be forgiven, as Carlyle forgives Lady Isabel, on the point of death. We are asked to feel acutely for the sufferings brought upon Sir Leicester by his wife's misdeeds, and to see it as appropriate that Lady Dedlock should die, literally, of exposure.

Neither Lady Isabel, tremulous and plaintive, nor Lady Dedlock, protecting her icy demeanour behind the firescreen, display much of the sexuality which might reasonably be supposed a characteristic of the fallen woman. Edith Dombey, on the other hand, though technically remaining unfallen, throbs with passion on every page. Where other women show feelings on their faces, Edith responds with her bosom. Carker, padding after Edith with all the silent relentlessness of Tulkinghorn, and Dombey, coldly imposing his will, have to contend with a good deal of anatomical antagonism. Mr Dombey is the first to experience the bosom's range of expression: when he attempts to exercise his authority Edith's disdain is signalled by 'her swelling breast', impatience by the 'diamonds . . . that rose and fell upon her bosom' and anger by 'the trembling lips, the throbbing breast'. At the mere mention of Carker's name 'her face and bosom glowed'; and as her horror mounts and the necessity of preserving an appearance of calm increases, the tell-tale bosom has to be restrained. She lays a hand 'heavily upon her breast' and is able to speak coolly: by 'raising the hand she pressed upon her bosom, and heavily returning it' she can let 'unusual feelings' slip out; and when she finishes speaking and the need for restraint is past, she 'dropped the hand with which she had enforced herself to be so passionless and distinct'. Carker is dauntingly met by 'a bosom angry at his intrusion' and a 'haughty breast', though both merely inflame his desire to steal her from her husband. Clearly Edith Dombey's involuntary sexual display is one of the marketable commodities so carefully nurtured by her grotesque mother and is thus a symbol of her shame and guilt. On the night before her marriage Dickens shows Edith in a frenzy of self-loathing: 'her broad white bosom red with the cruel grasp of the relentless hand with which she spurned it from her, pacing up and down with an averted head as if she would avoid the sight of her own fair person, and divorce herself from its companionship'.

This curious relationship with her bosom – quite how she goes about spurning it from her is difficult to conceive – is symptomatic of Edith's attitude towards herself as a woman and of the revealingly unsatisfactory case which Dickens constructs about the marriage market. At first it looks as though Dickens is making out the argument found in many of the New Woman novels – that marriage is too often a sordid financial bargain, that women are forced to deck themselves out to attract the highest bidder and to go through socially approved motions which are in essence shameful and degrading. This is certainly the line Edith appears to take in her bitterly sardonic description of her relationship with Dombey:

> He has bought me. . . . He has considered of his bargain; he has shown it to his friend; he is even rather proud of it; he thinks that it will suit him, and may be had sufficiently cheap. . . .
> . . . There is no slave in a market: there is no horse in a fair: so shown and offered and examined and paraded . . . as I have been. (*Dombey and Son*, ch. 27)

And the logical extension of this argument – that marriage is a form of prostitution – also creeps into the novel in the person of Alice Marwood, the prostitute and criminal whose finer feelings eventually ensure her a comfortable deathbed. Dickens seems to prompt us towards this conclusion when he asks rhetorically whether Alice and her mother 'were . . . only the reduction to their lowest grade, of certain social vices sometimes prevailing higher up'. But in fact the general application of this view of marriage is denied in two ways. Firstly, the sale of Edith to Mr Dombey is designed primarily as an illustration of the novel's main theme, the subordination of human affections to financial ambition, and in the end selflessness and generosity triumph sufficiently strongly to make the mercenaries appear as aberrations rather than typical representatives of human conduct. And secondly the suggestion that marriage is akin to prostitution is rather undermined when we discover that they are more specifically first cousins; Alice is the illegitimate child of Edith's uncle, and thus their extraordinary resemblance in character and behaviour is more a product of genes than of social pressures. Both are special cases, and need not be taken too seriously as comments on woman as a saleable object.

Nevertheless, it is interesting that Dickens links the direct sexuality of Alice Marwood with the outwardly respectable accomplishments of Edith, since it implies that sexual allure is as much a contrived commodity as the musical and artistic talents which are also put on display. Hence the bosom-spurning is a sign of Edith's guilt in taking part in the squalid matrimonial transaction and a recognition that her body is her most precious and most shameful asset. Though Edith finally spurns Carker more effectively than she does her own body, her physical presence is always potentially corrupting. Her marriage itself is described in terms very similar to a fall from sexual innocence, sprinkled as it is with intimations from Dickens that she would do better to die and followed by the characteristic shrinking from the touch of a pure young girl ('Is there anything unnatural or unwholesome in the touch of Florence, that the beautiful form recedes and contracts, as if it could not bear it!'). The flight with Carker is attended with slightly more extreme examples of the same kind of rhetoric – this time she 'had better have turned hideous and dropped dead' and 'crawled by [Florence] like some lower animal' – but her guilt is essentially of the same nature. Like all women who stray from the prescribed matrimonial path, Edith is denying the true feminine virtues as illustrated in the sweetly sexless figure of Florence. Female sexuality, the novel implies, is a mark of degradation.

Indeed, no novelist of the mid-Victorian period who wished to arouse sympathy for a fallen woman would risk portraying her as remotely sensual. It was difficult enough to argue that a woman could make such a mistake without being irredeemably corrupt in mind; to suggest that her body influenced her too would invite critical disaster. Mrs Gaskell's *Ruth*, in this period the standard fictional defence of the unmarried mother, depicts a woman of reassuringly ethereal beauty. Ruth falls, but rises so steadily through the course of the novel towards saintly purity that her inevitable death scene is attended with an embarrassingly awesome holiness.

Arthur Pollard, in his study of Mrs Gaskell, claims that she is trying to show how 'Ruth's downfall was a misfortune rather than a crime. To this end she insists on the innocence of Ruth'.[2] In fact what is most remarkable about this undisguisedly polemical novel in support of the fallen woman is that the victim's guilt is emphasised so heavily. Ruth is not guilty of being unfortunate but of sinning: the novel's argument, apparently innocuous, but severely criticised at the time, is that such a sin can and should be forgiven.

As in *East Lynne* there is a certain amount of confusion about the extent to which the woman should be held responsible for her actions but no doubt at all that the action itself is disgraceful. At first it seems that Mrs Gaskell is going to argue uncompromisingly that Ruth is to be viewed entirely as an innocent victim: she is barely sixteen years old when she meets her eventual seducer, Bellingham; Mrs Gaskell describes her as 'innocent and snow-pure'; we are coyly informed that her mother had died before giving her 'any cautions or words of advice regarding *the* subject of a woman's life'. Nevertheless, Ruth cannot altogether escape blame. Ignorance and inexperience do not provide complete excuses, for even girls such as Ruth, Mrs Gaskell suggests, have a sort of in-built early warning system which if heeded protects them from sin. After a walk with Bellingham which has left her with 'a beating, happy, agitated heart' Ruth reflects:

> How strange it is . . . that I should feel as if this charming afternoon's walk were, somehow, not exactly wrong, but yet as if it were not right. Why can it be? . . . There must be something wrong in me, myself, to feel so guilty when I have done nothing which is not right; and yet I can thank God for the happiness I have had in this charming spring walk, which dear mamma used to say was a sign when pleasures were innocent and good for us. (ch. 3)

The more sophisticated reader, who will already have Bellingham marked down as a seducer, is able to correct her judgement – her guilt, far from indicating something wrong in her, points to her fundamental righteousness – and can savour the irony of the innocent appeal to dear mamma.

Ruth does not listen to the inner warning, and Bellingham duly whirls her off to a life of sinful pleasure. The usual apparatus of regret and retribution creaks into action; her lover's ardour cools, the servants whisper maliciously, and a child delivers the conventional rebuke: 'She's not a lady! . . . she's a bad, naughty girl – mamma said so, she did; and she shan't kiss our baby'. Bellingham falls ill and is taken away by his mother, leaving Ruth broken-hearted and pregnant. Mr Benson, a dissenting minister of almost Christlike simplicity and virtue, deters her from suicide and summons his sister to nurse her back to health. The theme of redemption is put into motion; from this point Ruth moves towards a goodness of mind and soul which must make the ultimate denunciations of outraged respectability appear misplaced.

But again it must be emphasised that redemption can be effective only after a significant fall from grace. The guilt and shame following sexual transgression which Hardy was later to dismiss summarily in *Tess of the D'Urbervilles* as 'moral hobgoblins' are here integral to the theme. Despite all the mitigating circumstances, what Ruth did was a sin. 'I have deserved suffering' she says, with 'pretty earnestness', and the Bensons smile their approval; holding a child, she 'remembered that she was once white and sinless as the wee lassie who lay in her arms, and she knew that she had gone astray'; later, when the truth of her past life is revealed to the appalled inhabitants of Eccleston, Mr Benson declares that their hostility is 'but the reasonable and just penance God has laid upon you'. The point is not that Ruth's downfall is merely a misfortune, or that she is innocent of any crime, but that, as the repeatedly drawn parallels with Mary Magdalen indicate, her sin can be washed away. Mr Benson is the first to voice this argument:

> I can imagine that if the present occasion be taken rightly, and used well, all that is good in her may be raised to a height unmeasured but by God; while all that is evil and dark may, by his blessing, fade and disappear in the pure light of her child's presence. (ch. 11)

That the possibility of a fallen woman being raised again could barely be countenanced by the contemporary reader may be judged by Benson's reaction to his own words; so struck is he by the novelty of his sentiments that he trembles, weeps and indeed almost faints away. It takes him quarter of an hour, 'while he leaned back, exhausted by his own feelings', to recover.

Of course, there is little prospect of others being affected in the same way, so the Bensons reluctantly decide to pass Ruth off as a widow. This naturally involves them both in a certain amount of prevarication, and the fact that a minister should tell a lie was one of the things which most shocked the reviewers of *Ruth*. Mrs Gaskell too disapproves though on rather more subtle grounds than most of her critics. After the birth of her child, Ruth takes a post as governess in the house of the wealthy and upright Bradshaw family, and though growing steadily in goodness, and spreading sweetness liberally all around her, is doing so under false pretences. When Mr Bradshaw discovers Ruth's history and denounces her as 'disgusting', 'fallen and depraved', 'contaminating my innocent girls', he is not simply expressing a discredited conventional view. Mrs Gaskell assures us directly that Bradshaw has some cause for complaint: when he confronts Benson 'with a face glowing purple as he thought of his wrongs' she interjects 'and real wrongs they were'. In this instance Mr Bradshaw's judgement of character and fears for his

children are mistaken, but they may not have been. A sinner has
been smuggled into his household in the guise of an innocent widow
and he is not to know that she is already far on the road to
redemption. Mr Bradshaw is shown to be too inflexible in his
condemnation – he does not judge Ruth by what he has seen of her
character and behaviour, but only by the fact of her fall – but his
general point of view is not made to seem risibly extreme. He and
others like him must simply be made to see that it is possible for
sinners to return to the fold.

Ruth must now demonstrate her redemption publicly, and to this
end a typhus epidemic is made to strike the town. She volunteers for
the post of matron in the fever hospital, in the full knowledge that
she is likely to contract the disease and die. There is a curious little
scene in which Mr Benson gives his blessing to Ruth in what each
knows is virtually an act of suicide; her face shines with 'a bright
light . . . as of God's radiance'; and as stories of her sterling work
among the sick begin to spread, the poor people of the town are
marshalled to give final evidence of her spiritual elevation:

> Such a one as her has never been a great sinner; nor does she do
> her work as a penance, but for the love of God, and of the blessed
> Jesus. She will be in the light of God's countenance when you and
> I will be standing afar off. (ch. 33)

We might expect that the point has now been proved – a woman *can*
be both fallen and good. But a final grim twist is yet reserved. Ruth
does not die in the fever hospital. After the epidemic has slackened
and Ruth has returned home she learns quite by chance that one last
victim lies close to death. It is Mr Bellingham. Self-sacrifice and
forgiveness know no bounds; Ruth nurses him back to health,
catches the fever from him, and dies a beautiful death. The
sentimentality which has continually threatened to overwhelm the
novel finally floods in as the repentant sinner gains her reward:

> Suddenly she opened wide her eyes, and gazed intently forwards,
> as if she saw some happy vision, which called out a lovely,
> rapturous, breathless smile. . . . 'I see the Light coming,' said
> she. 'The Light is coming,' she said. (ch. 35)

Mrs Gaskell's case for the defence of the fallen woman carries the
implication that exceptional qualities and shining piety are needed

for her crime to be purged. Ruth is overpoweringly sweet and long-suffering; Mr Benson claims to see faults in her and refers to what is 'evil and dark' in her character, but it is exceedingly difficult for the modern reader to detect any blemish. Again we are forced back to the magnitude of the sin itself in order to understand the lengths to which a writer must go to evoke sympathy. Certainly even Ruth was not good enough to convince all contemporary readers that she merited compassion. Though the novel was well received in some quarters, enough moral outrage was generated to cause Mrs Gaskell considerable suffering. 'I have been so ill; I do believe it has been a "Ruth" fever',[3] she lamented to Miss Fox. But in one respect her attitude towards her own work was as conventional as the detractors could wish: 'Of course it is a prohibited book in *this*, as in many other households; not a book for young people'.[4] At this time her eldest daughters were nineteen and sixteen, both over the age when Ruth was led by her ignorance of the facts of life to commit the sin which finally caused her death.

The woman who fell, either before or after marriage, provided a striking and dramatic example of a flouting of the social and moral code. As we have seen, writers in the later part of the nineteenth century who wished to attack the code rather than the offender had an immense backlog of tradition to contend with, and the sort of precedent set by Mrs Gaskell was not really much help. But the New Woman writers were also interested in aspects of marriage which went beyond the stark sins of adultery or seduction. The whole structure of marriage as a way of regulating sexual relationships was to be dissected, and here again earlier novelists give useful indications of traditional assumptions.

That marriage should not be relied upon to provide a happy ending was conceded by a few novelists. In *Vanity Fair* (1848) Thackeray draws attention to his own originality in following Amelia beyond her wedding to the misery which ensues:

As his hero and heroine pass the matrimonial barrier, the novelist generally drops the curtain, as if the drama were over then: the doubts and struggles of life ended: as if, once landed in the marriage country, all were green and pleasant there: and wife and husband had nothing to do but to link each other's arms together, and wander gently downwards towards old age in happy and perfect fruition. (ch. 26)

But before Amelia can become properly aware of her mistake George is lying dead with a bullet through his heart, and her marital unhappiness is comfortably transformed into lachrymose widowhood. George Eliot probably went further than any previous novelist in the sensitive analysis of unsuccessful marriages, but her concern with her central characters is more for the complexities of their moral and spiritual ideals than for the mundane workings of social convention. The more commonplace aspects of marriage are better revealed by a novelist like Trollope, who, being adept at having the best of both worlds, acutely reveals the inadequacy of convention while ultimately reassuring his readers by making his characters conform to it.

Can You Forgive Her? (1864–5) is particularly interesting in that it deals with two closely related love problems and solves them, to the author's satisfaction, according to almost entirely contradictory principles. Alice Vavasor and her cousin Lady Glencora have both promised to marry men they do not love; the difference between them is that Alice has not as yet gone through the ceremony whereas Glencora has, and this difference proves crucial. Lady Glencora has been a victim of the sort of matrimonial managing deplored by the New Woman novelists. Dissuaded from marrying the man she loves, the poor and reckless Burgo Fitzgerald, she is pushed by the bevy of relatives ironically dubbed 'the sagacious heads' into a match with Plantagenet Palliser. Trollope's account of her relationship with a dry and unimaginative husband invites the reader to sympathise with Glencora. Palliser greets her with 'the embrace of a brother rather than of a lover or a husband' and gives her 'a somewhat longer lecture on the workings of the British Constitution . . . than would have been expected from most young husbands'. 'This total want of sympathy . . . this deadness in life', leaves Glencora with little to do but think of Burgo. 'Every hour of every day and of every night, – I am thinking of the man I love . . . I dream that his arm is round me,' she confesses to Alice, who responds sternly with the advice that 'she should be true to her marriage vow'. When she reveals her plan to run away with Burgo, Alice shudders with outrage: 'To her it was black in the depths of hell'. Trollope does not entirely endorse Alice's moral inflexibility, but has little to offer in its place. After Glencora's final rejection of Burgo, his comment is deliberately but infuriatingly ambivalent: 'She had had courage enough, – or shall we rather say sin enough, – to think of going with him. . . . But she was neither bold enough nor wicked enough to do the thing'. Characteristically, Trollope perceives Glencora's position as unjust and painful, but refuses to sanction a radical solution; the conventional judgement must be slipped in, if only in a tentative parenthesis. Lady Glencora has bound herself to a man she does not love, but must abide by the consequences; to do otherwise would be to sin.

This would not be so remarkable were it not for the parallel case of Alice Vavasor. At the beginning of the novel she breaks her engagement with the worthy John Grey, and, partly to please her cousin Kate, partly for the excitement of helping a man in his parliamentary career, accepts a proposal from Kate's brother George. However, she does not love George any more than Glencora loves Palliser, and Trollope makes it perfectly clear what he thinks about this:

> She had done very wrong. She knew that she had done wrong. She knew that she had sinned with that sin which specially disgraces a woman. She had said that she would become the wife of a man to whom she could not cleave with a wife's love. . . . She had thrown off from her that wondrous aroma of precious delicacy, which is the greatest treasure of womanhood. She had sinned against her sex. (ch. 37)

Of course this is precisely what Lady Glencora has done, and, in view of the pressures brought to bear by other people, with far greater excuse. Yet marriage itself proves to be an impassable barrier. Alice can redeem herself by the relatively simple expedient of breaking her engagement to George and reallying herself with John Grey. For Lady Glencora any attempt to rectify the sin involves her in further evil, is 'black in the depths of hell'.

It seems a peculiarly harsh judgement, one which if stated so baldly might stir rebellious reflections about the sanctity of marriage. Deftly but dishonestly Trollope smooths things over. Glencora confesses to her husband, who with unprecedented gentleness assures her of his love and forgiveness, and with a considerable effort of generosity gives up his dream of becoming Chancellor in order to take her on a tour of the continent. Sympathy is thus neatly shifted from wife to husband, Glencora is significantly in emotional debt and any further regrets about Burgo are made to seem selfish and frivolous. Finally she pays up with pregnancy, becomes 'the mother of the future duke'; and not all Trollope's comic ironies at the expense of Palliser's solicitude for the well-being of the embryonic heir can disguise the fact that the incident is crudely contrived as a reward for good conduct. Burgo is last seen destitute at a gambling table, and the 'sagacious heads' whose interference was satirised at the beginning of the novel turn out not to have been so foolish after all.

Clearly Trollope has dodged the crucial question: if it is wrong to become engaged to a man without loving him, why is it so patently right to remain with him after marriage? The lesson the New Woman novelist would derive from the example of *Can You Forgive Her?* is that marriage is at best an unsatisfactory, at worst an iniquitous, institution. Interestingly, this view is expressed in the novel by George Vavasor:

> 'It is a terrible thing to think of . . . that a man should give permission to a priest to tie him to another human being like a Siamese twin, so that all power of separate and solitary action should be taken from him for ever! The beasts of the field do not treat each other so badly. They neither drink themselves drunk, nor eat themselves stupid; – nor do they bind themselves together in a union which both would have to hate.' In this way George Vavasor, trying to imitate the wisdom of the brutes, had taught himself theories of a peculiar nature. (ch. 30)

George's argument, urbanely disparaged by Trollope, appears 'peculiar' here but is commonplace and approved in fiction thirty years later.

The woman who found herself miserable in her marriage in an early or mid-Victorian novel had little prospect of a second chance unless death conveniently stepped in to remove her husband. But what of the woman who had ambitions apart from matrimony? Early workers for women's rights were sometimes worth a passing sneer, particularly as their appearance was assumed to be as unattractive as their opinions. Thus in *Martin Chuzzlewit* we find 'a wiry-faced old damsel, who held strong sentiments touching the rights of women, and had diffused the same in lectures'; and in *Bleak House* there is Miss Wisk, 'a young – at least, an unmarried – lady' whom Esther 'cannot . . . report as prepossessing' and whose mission 'was to show the world that woman's mission was man's mission' and that 'the idea of woman's mission lying chiefly in the narrow sphere of Home was an outrageous slander on the part of her

Tyrant, Man'. The governess aroused more sympathetic feelings particularly when portrayed by writers who, like Charlotte and Anne Brontë, were speaking from bitter experience. But of course nobody became a governess out of conviction. The dedicated career-woman could not appear in fiction until careers were opened for her to pursue; all that we can look for in earlier fiction as a comparison to the New Woman's desire for independence and self-fulfilment is the comparatively rare treatment of the intelligent woman seeking useful occupation.

Charlotte Yonge's *The Clever Woman of the Family* (1865) is devoted to this theme and accurately reflects attitudes towards the intelligent and forceful woman which were common throughout the Victorian period. The novel opens with its clever heroine, Rachel, 'hauling down the flag of youth' on her twenty-fifth birthday. Ceremoniously (and not unwillingly) accepting the role of maiden lady, she makes a formal statement of her ambitions which would strike an instant chord of sympathy in the New Woman:

> Here am I, able and willing, only longing to task myself to the uttermost, yet tethered down to the merest mockery of usefulness by conventionalities. I am a young lady forsooth! – I must not be out late; I must not put forth my view; I must not choose my acquaintance; I must be a mere helpless, useless being. (ch. 1)

The business of this novel, however, is to deride these sentiments, a job which it accomplishes with brutal thoroughness.

Two sorts of antithesis are set up. The first is between the lumbering earnestness of Rachel and the intuitive femininity of her cousin Fanny; the second points the difference between Rachel's crass display of intellectual superiority, indicated mainly through her use of polysyllabic words, and the gentle and tactful intelligence of the long-suffering invalid Ermine Williams. Cleverness in women is not necessarily a bad thing, Charlotte Yonge implies, but it must be confined within strict feminine bounds, and preferably to a wheelchair where it cannot do much damage. Rachel, being mobile and having, as Ermine points out, 'no man nearly connected enough to keep her in check', sets out on a course of destruction. She begins on the recently widowed Fanny and her children, an unruly brood who respond to Rachel's attempts to tame and educate them with the sort of boisterous bad manners which show them to be healthily impervious to the influence of foolish spinsters. Mother-love is worth a wealth of book-learning, we infer, as Fanny's homespun wisdom is brought in to counter Rachel's outlandish judgements. 'Do you not agree with me, Fanny, that female medical men – I mean medical women – would be an infinite boon?' demands Rachel, to which her cousin quaveringly replies that 'it would be very nice if they would never be nervous'. We are invited to laugh not merely at Rachel's slip of the tongue, but more importantly at the image of a woman doctor conjured up by Fanny's unwittingly shrewd response. Nerves are an essential part of the female character; the novel is to prove that even Rachel has them.

Having failed with Fanny, Rachel turns her attention to the wider problems of women's employment. She writes articles on the female labour force, and stories in which the heroines end up in 'various industrial asylums where their lot should be far more beatific than marriage – which was reserved for the naughty ones to live unhappy in ever after'. All are firmly turned down by editors, who, it transpires, are too busy lapping up the columns of sweetly feminine insights churned out regularly by Ermine Williams to pay attention to Rachel's crude social commentary. This second failure is thematically acceptable: though we never learn exactly how Ermine's superior talents are manifested in print, the snippets we get of Rachel's efforts make it clear that she does not deserve to get published. But when Charlotte Yonge turns to Rachel's attempts at practical help the novel becomes more insidious in its message.

Rachel has long deplored the activities of the local lace-making school, which provides the only outlet of work for poor girls of the neighbourhood and is thus in a position to exploit its labourers. One day when scrambling down a cliff face to rescue a stranded dog – at least her physical skills are never in doubt – Rachel meets a Mr Mauleverer, who lends a hand with the dog and a sympathetic ear to her lecture on the plight of the lace-makers. Together they set up in a nearby town a residential establishment which will train girls in alternative skills and will finally realise Rachel's dream of helpful work in the cause of women. Unfortunately Mr Mauleverer is a professional con-man. The children under his care are treated viciously, starved and beaten, and – the final irony – employed in lace-making at rates which undercut the local school. Significantly it is the meek Fanny who exposes the fraud and sweeps the children away to be succoured with broth and prayers. The treatment is too late – or too ineffective – for one little girl, whose death is laid indirectly at Rachel's door. Women meddling in affairs beyond their scope, we find, bring disastrous consequences, no matter how laudable their motivation. Rachel discovers this at the official inquiry; Mr Mauleverer has absconded, and

> here was she, the Clever Woman of the family, shown in open court to have been so egregious a dupe that the deceiver could not even be punished. . . . It was as though all eyes were looking in triumph at that object of general scorn and aversion, a woman who had stepped out of her place. (ch. 20)

However, Rachel redeems herself in all eyes but her own by fainting away in the witness-box. What she takes to be the ultimate humiliation proves to her friends that there is real femininity in her after all – she is 'nervous'. Her rehabilitation as a woman can now begin, and we finally see her happily married and surrounded by children. It is noted with approval that she has stopped using long words, and her husband deals with her occasional reversions to type by the simple expedient of closing his eyes and sinking into a torpor. It is left for Ermine Williams to sum up the transformation by describing her with glowing satisfaction as 'a thorough wife and mother'. All the earlier nonsense about helping female labourers is forgotten, and Rachel has learned to direct her energies where they belong, in the care of her family.

There remains one more area of concern to the later New Woman novelists for which useful parallels may be drawn with earlier fiction, the general assessment of woman's character and potentialities. This of course is the largest and most amorphous area of all, but when approached from a late Victorian feminist standpoint could normally be resolved into a rejection of what society as a body considered 'feminine'. Ideas that could occupy whole chapters of violent polemic in a novel of the eighteen-nineties are sometimes slipped unobtrusively into works of a much earlier period. Thackeray's parenthetical lecture in *Vanity Fair* on the deceit necessarily involved in womanly submissiveness is a typical example of a male writer ruefully lamenting the results of an ideal encouraged by his sex:

> The best of women . . . are hypocrites. We don't know how much they hide from us: how watchful they are when they seem most artless and confidential: how often those frank smiles, which they

wear so easily, are traps to cajole or elude or disarm – I don't mean in your mere coquettes, but your domestic models, and paragons of female virtue. Who has not seen a woman hide the dullness of a stupid husband, or cover the fury of a savage one? We accept this amiable slavishness, and praise a woman for it: we call this pretty treachery truth. (ch. 17)

And George Eliot, most of whose considerable insight into her various women characters is too closely integrated into theme and plot to lend itself to the process of extraction, places the young Maggie Tulliver against a background designed to reveal the inadequacy of conventional assumptions about women. Having straight hair, brown skin and a keen intelligence, Maggie is a 'small mistake of nature', a 'comical' girl. Even her affectionate father finds her 'too 'cute for a woman' since 'an over 'cute woman's no better nor a long-tailed sheep – she'll fetch none the bigger price for that'.

But the novelist most often cited as an early pleader for the real nature of woman is of course Charlotte Brontë. Few critics of feminist persuasion have felt qualms about extracting and quoting with justifiable approval the heartfelt outburst from *Jane Eyre*:

Women are supposed to be very calm generally: but women feel just as men feel; they need exercise for their faculties, and a field for their efforts as much as their brothers do; they suffer from too rigid a restraint, too absolute a stagnation, precisely as men would suffer; and it is narrow-minded in their more privileged fellow-creatures to say that they ought to confine themselves to making puddings and knitting stockings, to playing on the piano and embroidering bags. It is thoughtless to condemn them, or laugh at them, if they seek to do more than custom has pronounced necessary for their sex. (ch. 12)

In fact, extraction is precisely what this passage is best fitted for, since it has almost nothing to do with the novel. Nobody suggests that Jane Eyre should spend much of her time in pudding-making; indeed when male characters do urge Jane to a course of action it is very remote indeed from anything that custom would pronounce necessary for her sex – Rochester wants her to become a kept woman in the South of France, and St John Rivers sees her as a martyred missionary in India. What *Jane Eyre* does tell us, in a less exhortatory

manner, about women is both more subtle and more compre-
hensive. The abiding popularity of this novel surely rests upon the
fact that it is the first and probably the best expression of the idea
that a woman can succeed in womanly terms simply because of her
intrinsic value. 'I will be myself', says Jane, and that self is devoid of
all the outward advantages usually judged necessary for success.
Poor, friendless and above all plain, Jane Eyre wins the love of a
man who has vainly combed the whole of Europe looking for
satisfaction. She snatches Rochester from under the nose of the
stately and beautiful Blanche Ingram and is valued by St John
Rivers above pretty little Rosamond Oliver. Her triumph, dis-
creetly subdued though it may be, could scarcely have been made
more complete; the novel feeds the fantasies of all women who have
ever felt less than complete confidence in their own allure.

Far more explicit in its statements about the nature of women and
their lowly social position is Charlotte Brontë's second published
novel, *Shirley* (1849). Here we find not only a wealth of bald
pronouncements on feminine nature, but also a significant thematic
grouping of characters according to 'male' and 'female' qualities. In
the first category we have the frequent sneers at women from Mr
Helstone, summaries of an entrenched male position:

> At heart, he could not abide sense in women: he liked to see them
> as silly, as light-headed, as vain, as open to ridicule as possible;
> because they were then in reality what he held them to be, and
> wished them to be – inferior: toys to play with, to amuse a vacant
> hour and to be thrown away. (ch.7)

To counter this there are the timorous sorties made by his niece
Caroline into the borders of feminist thought. She wishes 'fifty times
a day' that she had a profession, and in her loneliness and despair
indulges in long soliloquies which slide into orations on deprived
womanhood:

> Look at the numerous families of girls in this neighbourhood. . . .
> The brothers of these girls are every one in business or in
> professions; they have something to do: their sisters have no
> earthly employment, but household work and sewing; no earthly
> pleasure, but an unprofitable visiting; and no hope, in all their life
> to come, of anything better . . . their minds and views shrink to

nervousness. . . . Men of England! look at your poor girls. . . .
Fathers! cannot you alter these things? (ch. 22)

In the second category we have the very notable divisions of the
minor male figures according to their relative 'masculinity' of
character. The rough, forceful, domineering men – Helstone,
Malone, Donne – are unlikable; the meek Sweeting and gentle Hall
are portrayed as thoroughly praiseworthy. And this type of
distinction is present more strongly in the schematic grouping of the
four main characters: Caroline, sweet and submissive, devoted to
the tough and sometimes violent Robert Moore; his brother Louis
drooping with unrequited love for tomboyish Shirley Keeldar.

Shirley herself probably has greater claims than any of her
contemporary heroines to being considered an early form of New
Woman. She flirts with a masculine role – 'They gave me a man's
name; I hold a man's position', 'I read just what gentlemen read' –
and for the amusement of sympathetic onlookers can step prettily
into the part of the swashbuckling Captain Keeldar. She separates
fighting dogs as efficiently as she deals with the squabbling curates,
wields a pistol with confidence, and, when bitten by a supposedly
rabid mongrel, calmly cauterises the wound herself. Also, like many
New Women, she has much to say on man's false image of female
character:

> Men, I believe, fancy women's minds something like those of
> children. Now, that is a mistake. . . . If men could see us as we
> really are, they would be a little amazed; but the cleverest, the
> acutest men are often under an illusion about women: they do not
> read them in a true light: they misapprehend them, both for good
> and evil: their good woman is a queer thing, half doll, half angel;
> their bad woman always a fiend. Then to hear them fall into
> ecstasies with each other's creations, worshipping the heroine of
> such a poem – novel – drama, thinking it fine – divine! Fine and
> divine it may be, but often quite artificial – false as the rose in my
> best bonnet there. (ch. 20)

But by the end Shirley, and the whole tone of the novel, descend to
conformity. Caroline's feminist-sounding desire for a profession and
her concern for girls similarly situated turn out to be based solely on
the assumption that she will never marry. She wants work to take
her mind off Robert Moore, and when at last he discovers that he

loves her there is no more talk of governessing for her or general reform for spinsters. A levelling process takes over: Louis Moore shakes off his dejection sufficiently to summon Shirley to a French lesson, re-establishing their old master-pupil relationship and proving himself a man. 'I scared her', he gloats in his diary, 'it was right; she must be scared to be won', and after a brief but violent battle Shirley is tamed, melting into a sweet dependence – 'teach me and help me to be good. . . . Be my companion through life; be my guide where I am ignorant: be my master where I am faulty'. In contrast, Robert Moore, after stopping a bullet from one of his discontented labourers, tosses helplessly on his sick-bed calling for Caroline, and she proves her strength by fighting her way through blizzards and the disapproving Yorke family to come to his side. The extremes of male and female qualities are honed away to ensure a harmonious ending. Robert and Caroline move closer together, and Shirley and Louis, who have come dangerously close to role-reversal, lapse back into conventional attitudes. Though in the bulk of the novel Charlotte Brontë deliberately undermines stereotyped notions of masculine and feminine roles, the ending essentially represents a comfortable compromise.

Thus Charlotte Brontë, whose novels, perhaps more than any others of the period, reflect a persistent and in many ways revolutionary interest in the essential nature of woman, ultimately endorses the idea that a woman's highest achievement lies in the conventional concerns of love and marriage. Even Lucy Snowe, who by the end of *Villette* (1853) has attained an impressive level of independence and fulfilment through work, is felt to be cruelly thwarted in the most important area of her life; because marriage is denied her, she can never exchange her cold maiden name for that of her redeemer M. Emanuel, and her final state as white-haired spinster headmistress is merely one of chill calm. In fact, the most remarkable conclusion to be drawn from all these examples of mid-century novels – an admittedly selective, but, it is hoped, representative, sample – is that the general picture painted of women is so consistent. There seems to be little difference in the basic conception of female nature between the writers who are righteously upholding moral convention – Mrs Henry Wood, Charlotte Yonge – and those, like Mrs Gaskell, who attempt forcefully to challenge it. In major and minor writers alike we find the same fundamental assumptions: women's main concerns are those of love, the home and family; they are morally fragile, continually threatened with the fatal fall from the purity which defines their respectability; and any hint of sexuality is dangerous and usually damning. Marriage is to be regarded as final: if a woman voluntarily abandons it, she puts herself beyond the social pale; if the writer wants to give an unhappy wife a second chance, the husband must be killed off. And although such a generalised picture can never be complete, cannot do total justice to finer complexities or to the odd contradictory example, it has a sufficiently firm basis in fact to establish the overall characteristics of the conventions governing the Victorian heroine. Without some understanding of this background, the impact of the New Woman novelists and the intensity of their revolt cannot be properly appreciated.

2 The Fiction of Sex and the New Woman

'November 2. I spent the evening quietly with Carrie, of whose company I never tire. We had a most pleasant chat about the letters on "Is Marriage a Failure?"'[1] By the beginning of the 1890s, then, the great marriage debate had penetrated, via the daily press, to that bastion of lower-middle-class conformity, the Laurels, Holloway. Though Charles Pooter was doubtless happily unaware of the fact, the New Woman's assault on sexual morality was well under way. In 1888 Havelock Ellis, still at the beginning of his career as spokesman for the new freedom, had declared uncompromisingly: 'Sexual relationships, so long as they do not result in the production of children, are matters in which the community has, as a community, little or no concern'.[2] In 1890 Hardy, in his contribution to the *New Review's* Symposium 'Candour in English Fiction', had lamented the constraints imposed upon the novelist by the tacit censorship of popular taste:

Life being a physiological fact, its honest portrayal must be concerned with, for one thing, the relations of the sexes, and the substitution for such catastrophes as favour the false colouring best expressed by the regulation finish that 'they married and were happy ever after,' of catastrophes based upon sexual relations as it is. To this expansion English society opposes a well-nigh insuperable bar.[3]

This time he really was being overpessimistic. Six years later Mrs Oliphant enrolled Hardy in 'The Anti-Marriage League', that band of intrepid novelists who displayed a 'disposition to place what is called the Sex-question above all others as the theme of fiction'.[4] The fiction of sex and the New Woman had arrived.

The storm which finally shook Mrs Oliphant into her famous display of matronly outrage had really struck in 1893 with the

45

publication of Sarah Grand's *The Heavenly Twins* and George Egerton's *Keynotes*. But ominous rumblings could have been detected several years earlier. In 1883 the *Saturday Review* published a disparaging article on the modern heroine,[5] accusing her among other things of getting on in years – she is often 'twenty or over' – and of displaying an unmaidenly degree of 'frankness and zeal'. She is disappointingly lifelike, 'no more than an ordinary mortal', and, the most serious charge of all, in good health. The ideal heroine, we learn, has been lost forever because of modern woman's irresponsible desire to seek a cure for indisposition; the romantic fragility of the old style of heroine demanded that she should show 'all the symptoms of what at the present time is medically described as debility, and treated with iron, cod-liver oil and sea air'. Some of the novels of this period certainly portrayed women who, if not repellently robust, undoubtedly anticipated ideas of the New Woman. Olive Schreiner's *The Story of an African Farm* (1883) combined a sensitive and interesting account of life on the South African veldt with a good deal of rather self-indulgent rhetoric about the unhappy lot of women and the iniquities of the marriage system. An irretrievably silly novel by William Barry, *The New Antigone* (1887), created something of a stir with its anti-marriage sentiments, but eventually packed off its free-loving heroine to the security of a nunnery. Far more significant, in terms both of raising Hardy's 'insuperable bar' and of the new portrayal of women was the 'Ibsen boom'. *A Doll's House* received its first London production in 1889, with *Ghosts* and *Hedda Gabler* following in 1891. What *Punch* termed 'Ibscenity' – undisguisedly sensual women imprisoned in miserable marriages, the ravages of venereal disease, a wife slamming the door on husband and children – became also the stuff of the New Woman fiction. If such things could be put on the stage, they could certainly go into novels, and in the hands of New Woman writers could be turned into overt feminist propaganda.

The authors of what came to be known as New Woman novels were not consciously creating a distinct school of fiction and often pursued widely different lines of attack. However, some common characteristics can be identified which establish the general tone of the fictional New Woman. The central part played by education and reading is a good example. A fair number of New Women are Oxbridge trained – the heroine of Grant Allen's *A Splendid Sin* was at Somerville, his *Woman Who Did* at Girton, and Ménie Muriel Dowie's *Gallia* is the product of an unspecified Oxford college.

More important than formal education, though, are the heroines' reading habits. 'I never, never thought that she would live to quote books to her parents', wails the mother of Sarah Grand's Evadne, and certainly the New Woman's friends and relatives have to put up with a formidable barrage of literary allusion. In the course of *The Heavenly Twins*, admittedly an extremely long novel, Evadne gets through Mill, Fielding, Smollett, Zola, Daudet, George Sand, *Ruth* and *Madame Bovary*; and this only while she's feeling relatively fit – when nervous breakdown strikes, she strips the circulating libraries of light fiction as an antidote to intellectuality. Mill and Spencer are prescribed reading for any aspiring New Woman, literally so in the case of Emma Frances Brooke's heroine Jessamine Halliday, who, having an enlightened doctor, is treated not with cod-liver oil but with *The Subjection of Women*. Mona Caird in *The Daughters of Danaus* persuades us that Hadria's idea of a pleasant evening's entertainment is an impassioned debate on the works of Emerson and Thoreau, and George Egerton's heroines outshine all the rest by trotting out references to Strindberg and Nietzsche – whom they have, of course, read in the original. Even the newspapers can be pillaged for polemic: Gallia's elderly aunts, cautiously trying to make conversation over the teacups with their alarming niece, ask what it is in the paper that so absorbs her. 'In a tone of level indifference' Gallia reveals that it is a discussion on legalised prostitution – ' "My *dearest* child!" "Dear Gallia!" came from the ladies on the sofa.'

Uncensored reading was often held responsible for what was considered to be one of the New Woman's most unpleasant characteristics, an almost terrifying frankness about sex. Plain speaking was the ideal, and few of these heroines fell short of it. They built total honesty about their own physical responses into a cardinal principle and the exaggerated matter-of-factness of their tone was calculated to shock. 'Come here and sit down for a moment', Gallia orders the man she loves, 'I want to see how you make me feel.' (Actually she lets the side down at this point – he makes her feel that she wants to kiss him, but she loses her nerve.) Gwen Waring, in Iota's *A Yellow Aster*, makes a valiant attempt to establish the correct procedures for marital fulfilment: 'Touches and caresses and things of that sort bring thrills and shakes and trembles and flushes. . . . Well, I must practise touches and such, and hope for results; also, I must not let myself shiver and feel sick when I in my turn get them bestowed on me'. George Egerton's women, though, are more sophisticated in their techniques. The heroine of her story 'A Cross Line' deals with her husband's tedious conversation by biting his ear until she obtains the desired result: 'His eyes dilate and his colour deepens as he crushes her soft little body to him and carries her off to her room'. But most men confronted with a New Woman declaiming on sex are more baffled than aroused. Herminia Barton in *The Woman Who Did*, having taken a fancy to a man and lectured him for some considerable time on the importance of complete frankness and freedom, stretches herself sinuously on the ground: ' "I am yours at this moment. You may do what you would with me." . . . He drew back. . . . He scarcely realised what she meant'. However, the more sustained passages of sexual analysis with which these novels abound spring from more complex circumstances and are best treated in context.

Strictures against marriage, on the other hand, are often included almost as isolated epigrams. Mrs Oliphant was perfectly correct in pointing to the flood of anti-marriage propaganda which appeared in the early 1890s; she was wrong only in attributing to its authors organised subversive intent. Though the grounds for criticism often differed widely, a few examples of the sort of comments made on marriage certainly give an impression of determined opposition. Many are simply (unacknowledged) adaptations of Shelley's Notes on *Queen Mab*: 'Love is free: to promise for ever to love the same woman is no less absurd than to promise to believe the same creed'. Thus we find 'Promise to *do* or not to do, if you will; but promise to *feel* or not to feel – what a transparent absurdity!' (*A Splendid Sin*); 'to contract to feel or not to feel – what transparent absurdity!' (*The Woman Who Did*); 'as if any two people, when they are beginning to form their characters, could possibly be sure of their sentiments for the rest of their days' (*The Daughters of Danaus*); and, from Sue Bridehead, 'it is as culpable to bind yourself to love always as to believe a creed always, and as silly as to vow always to like a particular food or drink'. Less philosophical but closer perhaps to everyday reality is Jessamine Halliday in *A Superfluous Woman*: 'I think very few would be married if it were not for the flattery and triumph and the fuss of the wedding-day, and if there were anything else to do'. And the inevitable sexual sacrifice was one of the commonest causes of complaint: 'Man demands from a wife as a right, what he must sue from a mistress as a favour, until marriage becomes for many women a legal prostitution, a nightly degradation', says a recently separated wife in George Egerton's

Discords, while the mere thought of religiously sanctioned sex sends Iota's Gwen Waring into a state of almost catatonic horror: ' "Then this one-flesh business, this is a horrid thing. . . . This is maddening! . . . One flesh!" she murmured breathlessly. "One flesh!" ' It is indeed a far cry from Mrs Oliphant's ideal of marriage as 'that faithful union of Two upon which pure and progressive society is built'.

A final, and at first sight somewhat surprising, feature common to all New Woman novels is the heavy emphasis placed upon nervous disorder, disease and death. In works so passionately concerned to stir discontent with the established order, to exhort women to greater freedom of thought and action, it is perhaps odd to find such a relentless catalogue of catastrophe. Mental breakdown, madness and suicide are apparently the common penalties the New Woman must pay for her attempts at emancipation. True, only Grant Allen's Herminia actually succeeds in killing herself, but Jessamine, Evadne and Hadria all display serious suicidal tendencies. Many of the New Woman novelists seem positively to wallow in gloom. From *The Heavenly Twins* and *A Superfluous Woman* we gain the impression that all British Army officers, and a large proportion of the Peerage, are suffering from tertiary syphilis, and since these are the men who provide the socially desirable matches into which innocent young girls are pushed, the results give considerable scope for gruesome description. In *The Heavenly Twins* we are forced to witness the agonising deaths of Edith Beale and her child, victims of a syphilitic marriage. Jessamine Halliday, after marrying the diseased Lord Heriot, produces two deformed and retarded children who, in a fit of more than usually savage fury, bite and tear each other to death. Their mother then descends rapidly into madness. George Egerton's heroines are continually quivering with nerves, not surprisingly since they are often either alcoholic themselves or attached to drunken and sadistic men; one, in a story bleakly entitled 'Wedlock', maniacally murders her step-children. Only Gallia really manages to hang on to her sanity, and this, as we shall see, at a fairly high price.

The point is, of course, that the New Woman's ideals were far too advanced for her environment. These novelists were trying to do two things at once: firstly, to argue the moral and social case for a high degree of emancipation, and secondly to show how firmly entrenched were the creeds and conventions which oppressed women. In the first instance they were putting forward high-minded principles, in the second describing the stark reality of practice. Since the system is so pernicious, the odds so heavily weighted, it would be absurdly utopian, the argument goes, to portray a New Woman succeeding in her aims. Thus the common pattern of the New Woman novel is to show the heroine arriving at her ideals of freedom and equality from observation of her society, but then being brought through the miserable experience of trying to put them into practice to a position of weary disillusion. 'My ideal of perfect bliss in these days is to know nothing and believe in ghosts', says Evadne. Gallia, having finally agreed to marry a man for whom she has no real feeling, sneers cynically at her former self: 'What chatter it is to talk of being free, or of getting free! as if we ever could! Make her the moment and the man, and every woman takes to sentiment smiling, as a little yellow fluffy duckling flounders quacking to a pool!' And Hadria, with characteristic pithiness, sums up these feelings of defeat: 'A woman with ideals is like a drowning creature with a millstone round its neck. I have had enough of ideals'. Of course, the authors do not endorse their heroines' sentiments; the fact that women of such talent and intelligence are forced back into humiliating surrender is presented as yet further proof that the social fabric is rotten.

Contemporary critics who were not too blindly outraged to make any sort of discriminating judgement distinguished two main types of New Woman fiction. The first, dubbed by Hugh Stutfield the 'purity school',[6] comprised the works of Sarah Grand, Iota and Grant Allen; later they became known also as 'hill-top novels' after Grant Allen's sub-title to *The British Barbarians*, a hill-top novel, he explained, being one 'which raises a protest in favour of purity'. All these writers clung to the notion that there was such a thing as a feminine ideal, that women did occupy a different, though equally important, sphere, and that 'purity' was the highest principle. The catch was that their conception of purity was almost the exact reverse of everybody else's. Their main aim, in fact, was to discredit the old idea of the 'pure woman' which lay behind so many portrayals of Victorian heroines, and is encapsulated for example in this extract from *Lloyd's Penny Weekly Miscellany*:

> Matilda Rashleigh knew nothing of the world. Its cares, its blighting miseries, and its feverish short-lived joys were all unknown to her, – she lived in a world of her own – a world created by the purity and gentleness of her own heart – her ignorance was

indeed bliss. . . . Dream on, we would say to such gentle, trusting hearts as Matilda Rashleigh's; may it be long ere you awaken to reality when there is so much joy in the unreal. . . .

Far distant be the day when mock moralists or frantic philosophers succeed in blighting that first romance and beauty of existence which characterises the truly English girl.[7]

If Matilda, with ideas like these, had been rash enough to stray into a hill-top novel she would have found herself in no time at all with a dissolute husband, a syphilitic child, and a nervous breakdown. For these New Woman novelists, purity could derive only from knowledge, and possibly experience, of the world's blighting miseries, and if a few feverish joys could be picked up along the way, so much the better. Theirs was the purity of truth, personal integrity and freedom, and inevitably brought them into head-on collision with social convention.

The term Stutfield found for the second type of New Woman novel was the 'neurotic school'. This does not really tell us very much, since few New Woman heroines escaped neurosis of some kind; and in any case the works of George Egerton, Emma Frances Brooke, Mona Caird and Ménie Muriel Dowie are genuinely more diverse in their approach than the purity novels. Generally, though, their feminism was of a more radical kind, they placed greater emphasis on sexual freedom for women and were far less concerned with establishing an ideal of femininity. That a contrast was apparent to the public, though, may be judged from the argument between a pure and a neurotic heroine in Sydney Grundy's otherwise rather feeble satiric drama, *The New Woman*:

> Enid: And *I* say that a man, reeking with infamy, ought not to be allowed to marry a pure girl –
> Victoria: Certainly not! *she* ought to reek with infamy as well.[8]

Men reeking with infamy figure largely in the first recognisable novel of the purity school, Sarah Grand's *The Heavenly Twins*. Extracting the main themes from its 900 pages of close print and haphazard arrangement of incidents and characters is a difficult process, but basically its intention is to force a reassessment of the conventions governing female behaviour by portraying the most extreme results of conformity. It focuses on three women, each displaying a different response to an established order which is represented in the novel by their parents and almost the entire male population. The initial conflicts sometimes appear rather crude: Evadne, for example, has the mother who is reduced to tears by the thought that her daughter should quote a book at her, and who strongly supports the Matilda Rashleigh model of female excellence. She coos complacently over Evadne's marketable ignorance – 'I do know, however, that she is perfectly innocent, and I am indeed thankful to think that at eighteen she knows nothing of the world and its wickedness, and is therefore eminently qualified to make someone an excellent wife' – and views with alarm any attempt made by her daughter to rectify the situation. The parents of Edith Beale, the second of the main female characters, follow Evadne's in seeking nothing further for their daughter than respectable marriage to an army officer, and though all are perfectly aware of the sort of exotic sexual lives middle-aged men of this type are likely to have indulged in, they take the standard line that their daughters' purity and innocence will eventually elevate their husbands to an acceptable moral level. It doesn't seem to occur to them that even the most angelic feminine charm is no cure for venereal disease.

Fortunately, by the time Evadne comes to be matched up by her doting parents with the highly eligible Colonel Colquhoun, she has done enough reading to be able to protect herself. Her immersion in Fielding and Smollett has impressed her with the idea that their heroines are given short change in being expected to accept the hand of a charming rake, and she has also gained a rudimentary knowledge of the possible medical implications. When, immediately after her wedding, she receives a letter announcing that Colquhoun has led a life which would put Tom Jones and Roderick Random in the shade, she takes prompt action, giving her husband the slip at a railway station and rushing off to seek sanctuary with an understanding aunt. There then follows a lengthy, and on her mother's side increasingly hysterical, correspondence in which the case for and against the double moral standard is argued. This is where Evadne begins to come into her own as a heroine of the purity school, expressing herself with the sort of cogent irony and flat disrespect for conventional platitude which ideally characterise the New Woman. In reply to her mother's quasi-religious outpourings on the nobility of rake-reforming, she writes:

I am quite ready to rejoice over any sinner that repents, if I may rejoice as the angels themselves do, that is to say at a safe distance. . . . And, although reforming reprobates may be a very noble calling, I do not, at nineteen, feel that I have any vocation for it. (Book I, ch. 5)

Her mother's only response to this is to threaten her first with a lunatic asylum and then – more practically – with a suit for restitution of conjugal rights.

Sarah Grand then produces what at first appears a rather weak-kneed compromise: Evadne agrees to return to her husband, in order to avoid social embarrassment, on condition that there is no question of the marriage being consummated. In fact, this step is thematically necessary if the full conflict of Evadne's feelings is to be explored. The stand against her husband is taken partly on principle – if complete sexual purity is demanded from women, why should the same not apply to men – and partly out of regard for her own and her possible children's welfare. (She has before her the awful example of Edith Beale, who has married a man with a record as bad as Colquhoun's and has suffered the fate already described.) But Evadne, like most New Women whether pure or neurotic, has strong sexual feelings, and living under such conditions with her husband, an undeniably attractive man, puts her principles to the strongest possible test. Colquhoun is aware of this, and prepares skilfully baited traps by manipulating her reading matter:

He had arranged the books himself, placing Zola and Daudet in prominent positions, and anticipating much entertainment from the observation of their effect upon her. He expected she would end by making love to him. (Book II, ch. 1)

Evadne remains impervious to the inflammatory material of French fiction, but is often disturbed by her husband's physical presence. In one nicely contrived scene she accidentally encounters her husband among a group of friends and notes at first casually and then with quickened interest how physically superior he is to his fellow officers:

Evadne sighed. She was too highly tempered, well-balanced a creature to be the victim of any one passion, and least of all of that transient state of feeling miscalled 'Love'. Physical attraction, moral repulsion: that was what she was suffering from; and now involuntarily she sighed – a sigh of rage for what might have been; and just at that moment, Colonel Colquhoun, happening to look at her, found her eyes fixed on him with a strange expression. Was there going to be a chance for him after all? (Book II, ch. 12)

But these flares of sexual tension are quickly dowsed. Evadne might sigh with the rage of frustration, but she has 'perfect self-control': neither a French novel nor the tantalising glimpse of her husband in shirt sleeves – 'the most becoming dress a gentleman ever appears in' – will shake her into Colquhoun's bed. However, the control extends only to her body – her mind quickly begins to crack under the strain. The symptoms of her approaching break-down interestingly chart a progressive decline towards a position of feminine conformity; her madness is signalled by a return to what her mother would call sanity. First, she begins to take part in the social round, maintaining a dull politeness at tea-parties; then she stops reading dubious books and escapes into popular novels, and finally she starts to carp at feminism:

> I hear women say that they are obliged to interfere just now in all that concerns themselves because men have cheated and imposed upon them to a quite unbearable extent. But they will do no good by it. Their position is perfectly hopeless. (Book VI, ch. 1)

She retains, though, some faint traces of her former ironic manner – 'It is not high-minded to be neutral, I know . . . but a woman who is so becomes exactly what the average man, taken at his word, would have her be, and he is, we are assured, the proper person to legislate' – and this indicates to Dr Galbraith, one of the male proponents of feminism who are often allowed a bit part in a New Woman novel, that she is not beyond hope of cure. He takes up her case, treating her chronic depression and attempted suicide with large doses of sympathy, and finally recommending more formal psychiatric help. Sarah Grand is consciously parading her modernism in sending her heroine to London to be treated by a doctor of the new psychological school, but in the end this proves less effective than the death of Colquhoun and Evadne's marriage to Galbraith.

The third of the main female characters is Angelica, one of the twins who give the novel its title. The wild youthful pranks of Angelica and her brother provide some welcome comic relief, but also have a serious thematic purpose. Boy and girl twins, insepar-able in childhood and sharing the same courage, intelligence and talent, are forced as adults into utterly different moulds. Angelica weeps when she is first put into long dresses, and it is she who subsequently has most to say about the social conditioning of women into a role which, for many, is totally unsuitable. She is, for example, a brilliant violinist, but is discouraged from performing in any but the most amateur and trivial way. And it is Angelica who is allowed to expound at greatest length the novel's plea for female equality:

> I see where the mistake has been all along. There was no latitude allowed for my individuality. I was a girl, and therefore I was not supposed to have any bent. I found a big groove ready waiting for me when I grew up, and in that I was expected to live whether it suited me or not. It did not suit me. It was deep and narrow, and gave me no room to move. You see, I loved to make music. Art! That was it. There is in my mind an imperative monitor which urges me on always into competition with other minds. I wanted to *do* as well as to *be* . . . but when the time came for me to begin, my friends armed themselves with the whole social system as it obtains in our state of life, and came out to oppose me. They used to lecture me and give me good advice, as if they were able to judge, and it made me rage. I had none of the domestic virtues, and yet they would insist on domesticating me. . . . I had the feeling . . . that if I broke down conventional obstacles – broke the hampering laws of society, I should have a chance. (Book II, ch. 15)

Actually, Angelica's assault on conventional obstacles is conducted in a rather wayward manner. Far from attempting to avoid the groove of marriage, she actually proposes to a man, the staid and somewhat portly Mr Kilroy who has known her since she was a child. Admittedly, she does so under rather special circumstances. She has been present at the death-bed of Edith Beale, and is so shocked and distressed by this example of what can happen to the wives of dashingly attractive men that she rushes from the sick room into Kilroy's arms, and breathlessly orders him to preserve her from a similar fate by marrying her himself. Kilroy, slightly taken aback but not displeased, readily complies; only later does he discover the catch – Angelica cannot be married to anyone unless he agrees to let her do whatever she pleases, provided it is not immoral. What pleases her most, she finds, is to dress herself in her brother's clothes and steal out of the house at night to meet a romantic young man, with whom she achieves a strictly intellectual rapport. Though this transvestite adventuring is meant to have some polemical point – she wishes to 'see the world as men see it' – this part of the novel inevitably becomes rather strained. Sarah Grand is at pains to assure us that Angelica's nightly visits to the Tenor – so called because he is possessed of a beautiful voice and is lonely and mysterious – give her not the slightest sexual *frisson*, but she finds it difficult to explain away the Tenor's yearning for the oddly beautiful youth he takes Angelica to be. Certainly he is dismayed rather than thrilled when he finally discovers, in the course of rescuing her from drowning, that she is actually a woman, and listens rather bleakly as, by way of explanation, she gets once more into her feminist stride:

> I think it is dangerous to leave an energetic woman without a single strong interest or object in life. . . . I should have been held to have done my duty if I had spent the rest of my life dressing well, and saying the proper thing; no one would consider the waste of power which is involved in such an existence. You often hear it said of a girl that she should have been a boy, which, being interpreted means that she has superior abilities; but because she is a woman it is not thought necessary to give her a chance of making a career for herself. I hope to live, however, to see it allowed that a woman has no more right to bury her talents than a man has; in which days the man without brains will be taught to cook and clean, while the clever woman will be doing the work of the world. (Book II, ch. 15)

These days are too distant to be of any immediate benefit to Angelica, however, and she makes the best of a bad job by returning to Kilroy and surprising him once more by making the sort of passionate overtures which Colquhoun had vainly hoped to evoke from Evadne.

The Heavenly Twins, then, rests its case on the idea that the socially sanctioned modes of feminine behaviour are inadequate and indeed dangerous. Edith Beale is punished as savagely for conforming to the ideal of womanly behaviour as Lady Isabel Vane was for deviating from it. But in terms of sexual morality Sarah Grand manages to keep on the windy side of popular prejudice. Evadne and Angelica both have strong sexual feelings, but do not indulge them outside marriage: indeed both are finally left in domestic circumstances which, if not giving full scope to their intellectual potentialities, are at least sufficiently satisfactory to make them wish to stay. Certainly Sarah Grand herself had a stronger respect for marriage than any of the other New Woman writers: 'Women will always be women, and men always men', she informed an interviewer from *Woman*, 'and marriage, in my opinion, must always be the ideal state'.[9] Probably it was the novel's cunning combination of daring theories with eccentric but morally acceptable actions which made *The Heavenly Twins* such an outstanding success with the public. Though rather coolly reviewed on its first appearance, enough hints were dropped to suggest that there was more to it than could be revealed in a respectable paper. 'A daring novel', said the *Review of Reviews*;[10] one which 'explicitly or implicitly raises a number of quesions which cannot be adequately discussed in *any* column of a journal with a mixed *clientèle*',[11] explained the *Spectator*. Whatever the reason, the first edition was a sell-out within a month, and a few weeks after publication Heinemann were claiming sales of over 40,000 copies.

Sarah Grand's triumph was clearly an inspiration to other writers. Iota's *A Yellow Aster* (1894) opens with a description of a wild and uncontrollable brother and sister who are suspiciously reminiscent of the Heavenly Twins. Like Sarah Grand, Iota makes much of the fact that the boy can develop naturally into whatever he wants to be whereas the girl is dressed up and sent off to balls and dinner-parties. However, Gwen Waring grows into a far more alarming figure than any of Sarah Grand's heroines. She declares her intention of living life to the full 'without having my feet clogged with honey'; she has a masculine passion for riding hard over rough country; her lack of self-consciousness has 'an uncanny sexless sort of air about it', and she displays a 'brutal habit of speaking undiluted truths' especially about her response – or more often lack of it – to men. 'Gwen neither evaded nor shirked conventions, she simply swept them aside, as she did her lovers.' Her remorseless intelligence finds little to work on besides the analysis of her own emotions, and so, when the cross-country gallops become less fulfilling and she finds that tiresome men are forever proposing to her, she decides that it might prove an interesting experiment to marry. 'I like new sensations. I am curious.' But despite her worthy determination to 'practise touches and such' the hoped-for results are not forthcoming, and she finds that this is one new sensation she does not like at all. Her husband, aptly named Strange, decides to leave her alone for a while, but on his return Iota again follows Sarah Grand in making her heroine suddenly and mysteriously awaken to passion and settle down to a tolerable married existence.

The reception of *A Yellow Aster* in the press is interesting in that almost all reviews took Gwen Waring, despite her final conformity, to be a New Woman of a particularly unpleasant type, and many also saw the novel as part of the recent assault on decency in fiction. 'This New Woman differs from the old-fashioned woman in nothing but the absence of all regard for the feelings and comfort of others', said the *Critic*.[12] The *Bookman* used *A Yellow Aster* as an excuse to define and attack the new type of heroine: 'She is icily pure in her dislike of the marriage bond. She despises the world, and men, and herself, and is superbly unhappy. In spite of her purity she is not very wholesome; she generally has a mission to solve the problems of existence, and on her erratic path through life she is helped by no sense of humour'.[13] And the *Nation* was goaded into a long diatribe which, despite the sarcasm, showed a good understanding of what this and other novels of the purity school were doing:

A cardinal principle of our band of reformers, or inconoclasts . . . is that life can be purified only by delving for hidden impurity, by spreading it out for inspection, and, above all, by insisting that it shall be the subject of a searching analysis conducted in partnership by young men and women contemplating matrimony.[14]

This is quite right, of course: the aim of these novels was to show that purity could be based only on knowledge of life's darker facts, and they certainly encouraged plain speaking between the sexes, whether before or after marriage. The writer is also correct, though again extremely scathing, about the New Woman novelists' desire to liberate English fiction:

In default of any other justification, we are obliged to regard [*A Yellow Aster*] as the climax of effort for the emancipation of the English novelist from the yoke of the virgin. Fearless now of censure or of the diminution of sales, our novelists may proceed to tear away any poor shreds of decency that cling to and clog the skirts of society, restricted only by a careful assumption of a burning sense of their duty to the race.

In seeing *A Yellow Aster* as the climax of this effort, though, the writer is being hopelessly overoptimistic; far worse was to come, mainly in the form of *The Woman Who Did*.

It is difficult to escape the conclusion that Grant Allen was a man of somewhat limited intellectual and artistic capabilities. This is a pity, since his contribution to the New Woman fiction ultimately overshadowed all the rest and was remembered long after the works of his more sensible contemporaries had faded into oblivion. A classicist by training, a scientist by inclination, one-time professor of Mental and Moral Philosophy in Spanish Town, Jamaica, and a passionate reformer of whatever was commonly thought to need reform at the time, he was best known as a writer of eminently forgettable light fiction. 'Few living men', said Frederic Harrison in his funeral address, 'ever had so many irons in the fire – irons, be it said, of strange incongruity and divergence.'[15] Nobody doubted the sincerity with which he espoused each new cause, but some were forced to admit that his championship was often eccentric and sometimes positively damaging. This is certainly true of his support for female emancipation. 'I am an enthusiast on the Woman Question', he declared in an article for the *Fortnightly Review* in 1889.[16] Announcing that he has 'the greatest sympathy' with modern woman's fight for freedom he sets out a programme of reform which would effectively shackle her forever. Higher education for women is a most desirable thing, he says, so long as what they are taught is 'to suckle strong and intelligent children, and to order well a wholesome, beautiful, reasonable household'. 'Probably . . . even the most rabid of Women's Rights people', he states, with quite unwarranted confidence, 'would admit . . . that in the best-ordered community almost every woman should marry at twenty or thereabouts.' It is then her plain duty to produce at least four, and preferably six, children. But despite these apparently reactionary ideas, it was Grant Allen who went on to write what was often taken to be the most shocking, dangerous and revolutionary of all the New Woman novels.

What his woman did essentially was to have an affair with a man she was not married to. This had been done before, of course, but not usually on the grounds that any other mode of behaviour would be grossly immoral. *The Woman Who Did* (1895) bases its precepts on a neat and simple reversal of conventional sexual morality; now it is not adultery, but marriage, which is morally indefensible. Herminia Barton is to suffer 'martyrdom for humanity's sake' because of her determination to communicate and act upon this principle. Her mission is rendered unnecessarily difficult, though, by the fact that she (or rather Grant Allen) is unable to bring forward any sensible arguments in support of it. The novel is as full of empty rhetoric as *East Lynne*: 'I know what marriage is – from what vile slavery it has sprung', intones Herminia, 'I know on what vile foundations your temple of wedlock is based and built, what pitiable victims languish and die in its sickening vaults.'

Herminia's inspiration springs from the time when she hears her father, the Dean of Dunwich, giving a sermon on the text 'The Truth shall make you Free'; at this moment she resolved that 'whenever I found the Truth, I would not scruple to follow it to its logical conclusions, but would practise it in my life, and let it make me Free with perfect freedom'. She quickly gets the opportunity to begin when she meets her future lover, Alan: 'she liked the young man, and, the truth having made her free, she knew no reason why she should avoid, or pretend to avoid his company'. He, bemused by this treatment, and rather wilting under the bombardment of truth hurled at him, at first fails to respond, but Grant Allen makes another neat inversion of the expected to bring him into line. Herminia 'had power in her purity to raise his nature for a time to something approaching her own high level'; thus the old idea of a woman's moral superiority influencing men, attacked in its conventional application by Sarah Grand, is here used to wash away the stain of Alan's old-fashioned regard for marriage. The process takes some time to work, however, as Herminia discovers to her dismay in the middle of their first great love scene:

He folded her in his arms. Her bosom throbbed on his. Their lips met for a second. Herminia took his kiss with sweet submission, and made no faint pretence of fighting against it. Her heart was full. She quickened to the finger-tips. . . .

'So, Herminia, you will be mine! You say beforehand you will take me.'

'Not *will* be yours,' Herminia corrected in that silvery voice of hers. '*Am* yours already, Alan. I somehow feel as if I had always been yours. I am yours at this moment. You may do what you would with me.'

She said it so simply, so purely, so naturally, with all the supreme faith of the good woman enamoured, who can yield herself up without blame to the man who loves her, that it hardly even occurred to Alan's mind to wonder at her self-surrender. Yet he drew back all the same in a sudden little crisis of doubt and uncertainty. He scarcely realised what she meant. 'Then dearest,' he cried tentatively, 'how soon may we be married?'

At the sound of those unexpected words from such lips as his, a flush of shame and horror overspread Herminia's cheek. 'Never!' she cried firmly, drawing away. 'O Alan, what can you mean by it?' (ch. 3)

Though the main effect of this scene is – unintentionally – that of high comedy, it is still possible to discern the way Grant Allen's principles are working. Herminia retains the 'sweet submission' of the truly feminine woman, but combines this with a frank acceptance of – and indeed invitation to – passionate love. She can yield herself up 'purely' and 'naturally', but only to a relationship unsullied by the marriage tie; her 'flush of shame and horror' at the idea that Alan should wish to marry her is the exact equivalent of the conventionally pure woman's reaction to a proposal for an adulterous relationship. It is the ultimate inversion of the purity ideal.

Alan is finally persuaded to adopt Herminia's point of view, though with 'profound misgivings', and the two put the free-love plan into operation. Each is to retain complete independence – they live separately on the grounds that too much togetherness would breed intolerable boredom – and each is free to break the relationship at will. Even when Herminia becomes pregnant, the plan is not changed; she will continue to support herself by teaching and writing, and the child will divide its time equally between both parents. All this sounds laudably liberated, of course, but the impression is misleading. Beneath all this talk of independence and freedom lurks an almost entirely traditional ideal of femininity. Herminia 'was woman enough to like being led'; 'it is a woman's ancestral part to look up to the man; and she is happiest in doing it, and must long remain so'; and the stereotypes of sex roles are firmly maintained – 'the male, active and aggressive; the female, sedentary, passive, and receptive'. Even Herminia's career is not pursued for its own sake, since work is the least important of womanly activities: 'Every woman should naturally wish to live her whole life, to fulfil her whole functions: and that she could do only by becoming a mother, accepting the orbit for which nature designed her'. The fact that Herminia will remain self-supporting throughout her pregnancy and the child's infancy does not reflect an ideal, but the poor state of social organisation – government grants ought to enable the mother to be 'free to perform that function without pre-occupation of any sort'.

However, Herminia's martyrdom is not long in coming. She and Alan remove themselves to Italy for the birth of their daughter, where he quickly succumbs to typhoid and dies. The disadvantages of being sedentary, passive and receptive should then become apparent, though Grant Allen does his best to gloss them over with hyperbolically tragic images: 'She sat, a lonely soul, enthroned amid the halo of her own perfect purity'. Even the Truth is no match for a London landlady, and on her return to England Herminia weakly passes herself off as Mrs Barton. Her one remaining aim is to raise her daughter to succeed where she failed, and to this end she scornfully rejects all offers of financial aid from Alan's father. 'The child who was born to free half the human race from aeons of slavery must be kept free from all contagion of man's gold and man's bribery', Grant Allen explains. Instead Herminia turns to literature as a means of support, writing poetry which, from the example quoted, is clearly appalling, and a novel – 'It was blankly pessimistic, of course. Blank pessimism is the one creed possible for all save fools'. Certainly she has reason to feel gloomy: her daughter evinces a total lack of interest in freeing half the human race from slavery – indeed her one aim in life as she grows up is to get married as quickly as possible. 'Right and wrong meant to her only what was usual and the opposite', and when she gets engaged it is for Herminia 'the final thorn in her crown of martyrdom'. Pure to the last, she decks herself out in a white dress and two red roses, and puts an end to it all with prussic acid.

The fact that *The Woman Who Did* is, in literary terms, an extremely bad novel in no way affected its reception. It was the message, not the medium, which counted. Grant Allen himself, as one might expect, suffered no doubts about the artistic quality of his work, but did express fears that his views were too advanced for the times: indeed he made elaborate provision to preserve the manuscript in the event of its total rejection by publishers – after his death it was to be bequeathed to the Bodleian, whose custodians were to judge the proper time to bring it before the world. Even after the book was accepted by John Lane, Allen was writing pathetically to his friends, begging their help in publicising it: 'If it fails to boom, I go under for ever. I hope, therefore, you will talk about it to your friends, no matter how unacquiescently. It is a serious crisis for me, and only a boom will ever pull me through'.[17] His worries were entirely groundless; *The Woman Who Did*, coming to a public already warmed up by the earlier New Woman novels, and eager for further stimulation, whether to outrage or reforming zeal, hit exactly the right note and boomed beyond anybody's wildest dreams. The novel ran through nineteen editions in one year, gave rise to innumerable jokes along the lines of Women Who Wouldn't, Women Who Wanted To and Women Who Would if they Could, and coined Allen £1000 a year in royalties until his death in 1899.

Flushed with his own success, Grant Allen produced a few months later another work containing the free-love, anti-marriage theme, *The British Barbarians*. Though this is in every respect a better novel than *The Woman Who Did*, mounting its attack on social convention with satire and irony rather than inflated rhetoric, it is chiefly notable for coining the 'hill-top' label. 'A Hill-Top Novel' stands portentously as sub-title, and was chosen, with typical literalness, because the novel was written in a house situated on top of a hill. In a lengthy and somewhat pompous Preface, Allen explains the meaning of the term. He hits out at editors and circulating libraries for making it impossible for novelists to 'proclaim to the world at large the things which they conceive to be best worth their telling it'. Conceiving himself to be the advance guard of a movement which actually had at least two years' start on him, Allen announces his intention of writing freely and openly about, among other things, sexual morality. With a fine flourish he declares that he will sacrifice three-quarters of his income (which would otherwise come from serial rights) 'for the sake of uttering the truth that is in me, boldly and openly, to a perverse generation', but since *The Woman Who Did* probably made him more money than all his serialised trivia put together, this is an obviously hollow gesture. However, other writers are invited to follow him in producing novels in which the truth shall appear as 'fresh and pure and wholesome' as the air of the hill-top. Undoubtedly Grant Allen's posturing had a very bad effect on the market. Although the 'hill-top' label had a brief vogue – it was frequently attached, for example, to *Jude the Obscure* – Allen was attacked so vigorously and consistently that saner novelists natually became wary of exposing themselves to the charge of following in his footsteps. The *Spectator* devoted a whole article to ' "Hill-Top" Novels and the Morality of Art', lining up all the purity school works, and some other novels of dubious morality, for violent denunciation: 'The novels which, in the name of purity, aim blow after blow at all the safeguards of purity, are unhappily very numerous. They make the class for which we were wanting a common name, and we are glad to escape the responsibility of coining one that might have given offence, by adopting that which Mr Grant Allen has invented'.[18] In fact this was not necessary; Allen's efforts effectively put an end to the purity school of New Woman fiction, and the hill-top novel died more or less at birth.

The first work of the neurotic school, George Egerton's *Keynotes*, appeared a few months after *The Heavenly Twins* and enjoyed comparable success. Stutfield found 'much that is pathetic in the self-questioning and the craving of the type of woman depicted in neurotic fiction. There is a note of infinite weariness, a kind of anaemic despondency, in books of the *Keynotes* class; but there is also a note of real pain'.[19] Certainly the New Women in this type of novel, though differing widely in some aspects, rarely display the haughty self-confidence or spirited revolt of the purity school heroines. Nobody would accuse them of being 'icily pure'; they were far closer to the 'intellectualised, emancipated bundle of nerves' identified by the German reviewer of *Jude the Obscure* as the type to which Sue Bridehead belonged. George Egerton adopted, both in life and fiction, a far more sophisticated attitude towards sexuality than Sarah Grand and her followers. Writing to her father about the first London production of *Ghosts*, she said:

> I am afraid my sensibilities are blunted, considering that every little hospital nurse knows of the existence of syphilis, every married woman and a large number of unmarried ones, and that every day's paper has a 'horror' of some kind or other, I don't see where the shockingness comes in. . . . I don't like Ghosts, particularly in a raw translation, but I see more to be shocked at in one walk through the Strand or Leicester Square, let us say, at 11 pm.[20]

Clearly she is to some extent exaggerating for effect, showing off the fruits of her own experience, but since it is difficult to think of many other writers of the period who would feel able to offer comments on the quality of a translation from Norwegian she has some justification for feeling superior.

This worldly-wise tone, which also informs much of her fiction, is something to which she had undoubtedly earned a right. Her stories are based largely on personal experience, and this was sufficiently varied and outlandish to give almost infinite scope for shock. Born in Australia of an Irish father and a Welsh mother, she was educated for some time in Germany, trained as a nurse, and took off to earn her own living in America before finally coming to England. When a newly married couple invited her to form a threesome with them in their travels she accepted with alacrity and, taking them rather literally at their word, began an affair with the husband. She and the man, unromantically named Henry Higginson, went off to live in Norway, where George Egerton learned the language and became steeped in the literature. She also learned, from Higginson, rather more than she had bargained for about alcoholism and violence, but got her own back by using him as a model for some of the men in her stories. After Higginson's death she married an idle, destitute Canadian, with whom she lived in Ireland until her career as a writer took her to London and the arms of various literary figures including, it seems, John Lane and Richard le Gallienne. She divorced her husband in 1901, married again the same year, and worked as a journalist and as a dramatic agent for, among others, Shaw, Somerset Maugham and J.M. Barrie. All in all, she was an interesting woman.

She began to write short stories as a means of supporting her first husband and, after sending them to Heinemann and having them refused, had the good sense to follow them to the Bodley Head offices in person, where she made an immediate impact as 'a very attractive young woman, slim, dark-haired, and dressed all in white'.[21] So impressed was Lane – by the stories as well as their author – that he made *Keynotes* the first of a special series which was to bear its name and carry the élite of the Bodley Head writers (*The Woman Who Did* and *The British Barbarians* were both 'Keynotes' novels). Lane commissioned Aubrey Beardsley to design a special cover for *Keynotes* – 'between pale pink and mauve' – and though this had to be suppressed to calm the nerves of the circulating libraries, Beardsley tried again and produced more subdued covers for all the novels in the series. George Egerton was wafted effortlessly to fame on the air of the decadent nineties, and had the distinction of appearing in the first issue of *The Yellow Book*.

It is difficult to capture the tone of her stories. Though she has some irritating stylistic mannerisms, relying too heavily on present tense narration, and striving for an economy of effect which often falls into the merely perfunctory, she does clearly display some literary sensitivity. Almost all the stories deal with some aspect of female sexuality, but on the whole without the stridency, and consciousness of being perversely daring, which mar the works of Iota or Grant Allen. Her heroines are far removed from the polite social circles in which Sarah Grand's were placed, hovering in the twilight world of the alcoholic, the kept woman or the lonely divorcee. Her plots are based on the fleeting moment, the sudden significant incident in a tangle of human relationships, and though there is little direct feminist polemic she is more genuinely original in her portrayal of the female character than any writer of the purity school. If one main discursive theme can be singled out from the diversity of her work, it is that women are by nature extremely sensual and that it would be as well if this were generally recognised. Men 'have overlooked the eternal wildness, the untamed primitive savage temperament that lurks in the mildest, best woman', she says in *Keynotes*. 'You see there is no time of sowing wild oats for women; we repress, and repress, and then some day we stumble on the man who just satisfies our sexual and emotional nature, and then there is shipwreck of some sort.' Occasionally she will bring on some of the New Woman props – a cigarette, a bicycle, a French novel – and some stories deal with the consciously emancipated wife: 'My husband stays at home and grows good things to eat, and pretty things to look at, and I go out and win bread and butter'. But the main impact of her work lay in its depiction of the sensual woman for whom 'purity', of whatever kind, was an irrelevance. The lengthy and elaborate sexual fantasies which many of her *Keynotes* heroines enjoy could have no place in a purity novel:

> She can see herself with parted lips and panting, rounded breasts, and a dancing devil in each glowing eye, sway voluptuously to the wild music that rises, now slow, now deliriously wild, seductive, intoxicating, with a human note of passion in its strain. She can feel the answering shiver of feeling that quivers up to her from the close audience. . . . One quivering, gleaming, daring bound, and she stands with outstretched arms and passion-filled eyes, poised on one slender foot, asking a supreme note to finish her dream of motion. And the men rise to a man and answer her, and cheer, cheer till the echoes shout from the surrounding hills and tumble wildly down the crags. ('A Cross Line')

Even Herminia Barton never invited her Alan to this sort of orgasmic indulgence.

'Perhaps not the best kind of thing to recommend as a solace to the leisure of the curate's sister',[22] commented the *Bookman* cautiously, but despite a few predictable accusations of immorality *Keynotes* was favourably reviewed. 'Some woman has put her soul into this book', said the *Review of Reviews*, 'some woman has crystal-lised her life's drama, has written down her soul upon the page.'[23] Although the stories were universally said to be 'daring', it was the stripping of the soul rather than the body which impressed the reviewers of *Keynotes* and for a time George Egerton was the acknowledged expert on the inner workings of woman's nature. She followed *Keynotes* with *Discords* (1894), which also sold extremely well, but there was a limit to how long the theme could be played. *Symphonies* (1897) and *Fantasias* (1898) were far less successful, and in the end George Egerton found herself hopelessly out of tune with popular taste.

However, her exploration of female sexuality gave the lead to other writers who wished to integrate it more closely with feminist themes. Emma Frances Brooke's *A Superfluous Woman* (1894) shows an initially conventional girl awakening to sexuality and as a result being torn between her own desires and the demands of the high society in which she is brought up. 'Lovely women were bought and sold in the London marriage market very much as Circassian slaves are sold to a Turkish harem', we are told, and Jessamine Halliday, the superfluous woman of the title, has been taught to think of herself simply as 'a dainty piece of flesh which some great man would buy'. The depiction of upper-class society is flattened out to expose its vices at their crudest, but an enlightened opposition is also present, led by a doctor of feminist persuasion much like Sarah Grand's Galbraith. In the early part of the novel he and his like-minded friends spend a great deal of time in rather stilted discussion of conventional female behaviour and possible means of revolt for which Jessamine is later to provide the living model:

'You perceive . . . what a flat catalogue of conventional virtues we impose upon women, assuming them to be characteristics of the whole sex?'
. . . 'The manner of a woman's thoughts, deeds, and words is prescribed, as you say, beforehand by society; her very love must

be according to platitudes and the code. It must be a beautiful fidelity, affection, sentiment, but not a passion like a man's. But supposing a woman fall into something indecorously natural?' (Vol. I, ch. 2)

Jessamine's function is to give an example of how much more desirable the indecorously natural is. Emma Frances Brooke is not an author who shirks extremes. We first see Jessamine being reduced progressively to nervous illness by the emptiness of the social round, and though Dr Cornerstone props her up temporarily with his prescriptions of Mill she finally takes the cure into her own hands and runs away to seek independence and freedom among simple crofters in the Highlands. She escapes from being on the brink of engagement to the ageing and diseased Lord Heriot – 'the greatest catch in Europe' – only to find herself plunged into a hopeless passion for the 'noble peasant' Colin Macgillvray. Judged by the kindly farming family who give her lodgings to be 'as pretty as an Academy picture, and about as real' Jessamine must painfully unlearn all the refined graces which made her successfully tempt Lord Heriot and turn herself into a useful companion for Colin. Her first opportunity to prove herself comes when she helps him round up a flock of strayed sheep:

> It was the first time Jessamine had tasted real comradeship with a man. Comradeship is impossible where sex is predominant, and in the refined world which she had forsaken sex stands opposite to sex, the stronger with the stirrings of an exhausted sensuality, the weaker comporting itself as a *récherché* morsel which knows its price. But here all was changed. This stalwart peasant saw her only as a serviceable human being; he shouted orders in a peremptory tone as he ran hither and thither, and she made every effort to obey them, sending back shrill retorts when necessary, her voice forsaking in the exigency of the moment that sweet lowness which is an excellent thing in drawing-rooms. (Vol. I, ch. 8)

The process of abandoning decorum for the natural can then be extended from action to feeling. Jessamine slowly awakens to an understanding of sexuality – in one scene, whose crudity of symbolism would not have disgraced Lawrence, Colin snatches her from under the horns of a rutting stag and carries her home in his arms – and she begins to analyse her own responses:

> She had been instructed . . . into the duty of a girl to repress feeling, to hold herself poised between relative advantages until the event culminated from the outside. As to her own nature, of that she had heard nothing; passion, she had been taught, was an offensive word, an unladylike allusion. . . . What she was feeling might be right or wrong, decorous or indecorous; *that* was not the point. She partly realised that she did feel, that her heart, hitherto cold and virginal as snow, was melting and opening beneath an influence that was as new as it was strange. (Vol. I, ch. 10)

Unfortunately she is prepared to abandon herself to sensuality a good deal more freely than Colin, who, though unrelentingly noble, is also austerely religious and holds out for marriage. Jessamine's rather vague plan for conceiving his child and returning to London triumphantly pregnant and unmarried thus comes to nothing. The novel becomes irritatingly ambiguous at the crucial point: terrified – understandably – of committing herself to a man so different from herself, Jessamine vacillates nervously until the author brings events to a climax by, as far as one can tell through the fuzziness of the writing, making her attempt to seduce Colin. It is clear enough that whatever her aims she failed, for she is next seen back in London as the wife of Lord Heriot, being punished with the two murderous children and her own approaching madness. Dr Cornerstone and his circle continue to sit in wise judgement on the deplorable situation of women in society while Jessamine fights a losing battle with 'The Thing' which torments her in her deranged hallucinations.

Though the novel is fatally flawed by taking its case to patently ludicrous extremes, what Emma Frances Brooke is trying to do is reasonably clear. She wants to show both the inadequacy of woman's role in society and the impossibility of escape; Jessamine's discovery of sex, emphasised as theoretically important for emancipation by the Cornerstone clique, can find no outlet between the polarities of raw peasantry and corrupt aristocracy. The case is put too crudely, but the theme was a common one in New Woman polemic, and is far better handled by Mona Caird.

The Daughters of Danaus (1894) is one of the few New Woman novels which successfully integrates the demands of art and propaganda. Mona Caird already had a considerable reputation as a feminist and a journalist of formidable argumentative power. (One of the other things she cared about was vivisection, and she wrote as passionately about the exploitation of animals as about that of women.) She already had a couple of novels with feminist leanings to her credit, but it was in *The Daughters of Danaus* that she really launched into New Woman polemic. The significance of the title is that Danaus' fifty daughters, victims of an arranged mass marriage, were punished for murdering their husbands by being forced eternally to indulge in the fruitless labour of drawing water from wells with a sieve, and although Mona Caird does not positively advocate homicide as a means of escaping a bad marriage, she is concerned to show that laudably independent action is inevitably doomed by social constrictions to failure, and its perpetrators consigned to the everlasting pointlessness of feminine conformity. It is a bleak, but in many respects a perceptive and highly credible, analysis of a New Woman's situation.

The novel reverses the geographical progress of *A Superfluous Woman*, opening in the Highlands where Hadria, the central character, has already reached the point of feminist awareness which Jessamine took so long to attain. Mona Caird puts into Hadria's mouth many of the ideas about the social conditioning of women which had already appeared in her articles:

> Girls . . . are stuffed with certain stereotyped sentiments from their infancy, and when the painful process is completed, intelligent philosophers come and smile upon the victims, and point to them as proofs of the unvarying instincts of the feminine creature. (ch. 3)

But a novel offers greater scope for revealing the way conditioning can work even on a woman aware of the process, and Hadria's decline into matrimony is convincingly charted. Having come to rely heavily on the emotional and intellectual stimulus of her brothers and sister, she sees them one by one leave home – her sister Algitha is converted by Hadria's feminist arguments and goes to London to do social work – and she finds herself without congenial company in a dreary middle-class society. Her mother, prostrated by Algitha's rebellion, clings desperately to her remaining daughter, and for Hadria marriage offers the only means of escape which would not inflict intolerable pain on her parents. Thus when a more than presentable man appears and presses her to start a new life with him in England, resistance becomes increasingly difficult: 'The magic of personal influence had begun to tell upon her. . . . A temptation to give the answer that would cause pleasure was very strong'.

Mona Caird does not have to resort to the extremes of disease-ridden peers and maniacal offspring to convince us that Hadria's marriage is unhappy, and this of course makes the polemical point stronger. Hubert Temperley would be an ideal husband for somebody, but not for Hadria, and the breakdown of their marriage is described convincingly but in temperate terms. However, while Hubert's main concern is to save social face and protect the children, Hadria looks back to her earlier feminist ideals to provide a solution. At first she is tormented by the horrifying thought that there is indeed something innate in female nature which drives even the most emancipated women into marriage and pens them there for good:

> She must have been mad! The universal similarity in the behaviour of girls, herself included, alarmed her. Was there some external will that drove them all, in hordes, to their fate? (ch. 18)

But then she pulls herself together and decides for once to act on principle and leave husband and children in order to pursue her own career. Like Angelica, she is an accomplished musician, but Mona Caird deliberately nudges her ambitions further into male preserves by making her lean towards composing rather than performing. Hadria goes to Paris to study music and for a time revels in her freedom and self-fulfilment, ignoring all her husband's irate demands for a return to respectability. But when her mother, overcome with the shame of the situation, falls into the sort of convenient illness whose only cure is complete absence of worry, Hadria is forced to recognise that her freedom cannot be won without bloodshed. Faced with the 'bitter choice between unconditional surrender, and the infliction of pain and distress' she capitulates and returns home.

On the whole Mona Caird captures the importance of this sort of psychological pressure well. The situation she describes is far closer to the common pattern of middle-class life than that of most New Woman novels, and is thus, perhaps paradoxically, a more convincing incitement to revolt. The one thing which might at first seem rather odd is that Mona Caird should have selected Hadria's mother rather than her children as the main focus of emotional blackmail, but this is necessary in order to isolate one area of the novel's argument which is unique in New Woman fiction, its attack on the most sacred and cherished of all Victorian ideals about women, the maternal instinct. 'A woman with a child in her arms is, to me, the symbol of an abasement, an indignity, more complete, more disfiguring and terrible, than any form of humiliation that the world has ever seen', says Hadria. This sounds pretty extreme, though Mona Caird does allow the proviso that 'free motherhood', existing 'apart from the enormous pressure of law and opinion', would be acceptable. The reasons she makes Hadria give for her point of view are, however, basically sensible – it is, as she says, extremely difficult to be an emancipated mother:

> Throughout history, she reflected, children had been the unfailing means of bringing women into line with tradition. Who could stand against them? They had been able to force the most rebellious to their knees. An appeal to the maternal instinct had quenched the hardiest spirit of revolt. No wonder the instinct had been so trumpeted and exalted! Women might harbour dreams and plan insurrections; but their children – little ambassadors of the established and expected – were argument to convince the most hardened sceptics. Their helplessness was more powerful to suppress revolt than regiments of armed soldiers. (ch. 20)

It seems that this was one spin-off from the Anti-Marriage ideal from which even Grant Allen retreated in alarm: 'Herminia was far removed indeed from that blatant and decadent sect of "advanced women" who talk as if motherhood was a disgrace and a burden, instead of being, as it is, the full realisation of woman's faculties, the natural outlet of woman's wealth of emotion'. No doubt Mona Caird would have retorted that this proved her point.

Hadria is more typical of the neurotic New Woman in her attitude to sex. While still at liberty in Paris, she is confronted by her husband's sister, Henrietta, sent out by the family in the vain hope that a little womanly chat will soon bring Hadria home. Henrietta makes the mistake of complimenting her sister-in-law on the fact that, though possibly eccentric, she is obviously not the sort of woman to have affairs. Hadria whips round on her:

'You think I would regard myself as so completely the property of a man whom I do not love, and who actively dislikes me, as to hold my very feelings in trust for him? Disabuse yourself of that idea, Henrietta. I claim rights over myself, and I will hold myself in pawn for no man.'

Henrietta covered her face with her hands.(ch. 36)

Unfortunately Hadria is hauled back to England before she gets the opportunity to taste her sexual freedom, and after her return sinks into the apathy and mental disorder typical of so many defeated New Women. As she loses her faith in feminism, she begins to dilute the free-love ideal with the unprincipled but more conventionally feminine exercise of sexual power:

It is less than worthless. But I am not seeking anything of permanent value; I am seeking excitement, and the superficial satisfaction of brandishing the weapon that everyone would be charmed to see me lay in the dust. I *won't* lay it down to please anybody. (ch. 41)

This is the final flourish of aggression, though. The man she chooses to flirt with turns out to have seduced and abandoned the mother of an orphan child whom Hadria had adopted after the woman's death, and with one last burst of feminist power she rebukes and rejects him. Hadria sees herself as a humiliating example of defeat: 'how feeble after all are these pretentious women of the new order, who begin by denying the sufficiency of the life assigned them, by common consent, and end by failing in that and the other which they aspire to'. The male mentor who has hovered in the background throughout the novel, here a professor rather than the more usual doctor, dies urging Hadria to keep faith with her ideals, but the novel ends on a relentlessly depressing note. *The Daughters of Danaus* attempts with some success to combine an argument for the necessity of revolt with an analysis of why under present conditions revolt is bound to fail; its aim is to urge the more general change in social attitudes which would make success in the future possible.

Ménie Muriel Dowie's *Gallia* (1895) also takes a fairly gloomy view of things, but comes up with a rather startling solution. This author too had impeccable credentials as an emancipated woman, though she had won her spurs in more remote fields than Mona

Caird. Her first book, *A Girl in the Karpathians*, describes her solitary adventurings in this part of the world and is adorned with illustrations of the author dressed in tight trousers and thigh boots. It is a lively and interesting work, and those critics who unkindly expressed doubts about its veracity were unable to bring forward any evidence besides their own prejudices. *Gallia*, though set more conventionally in England and Paris, also emphasises the importance of courage and physical toughness for women, but its main message is that the road to freedom starts only from total, indeed ruthless, honesty about sex.

Gallia herself has a good emotional and intellectual background for this. Never having played with dolls as a child, she feels herself naturally deficient in femininity and grows up first to resent and then to make a principle of ignoring the conventional reticence demanded of women. Having had the benefit of an Oxford education she is able to break the silence barrier with some cogency. As we have seen, she refuses to spare her elderly relatives the full particulars of her – academic – interest in prostitution, and the same highly principled frankness is applied to her relationships with men. When she falls in love with the dark and dashing Essex, she takes him aside and explains the fact to him in some detail, only to be met with a stiff rebuke: 'Don't you think the world is still a little too raw for your very advanced treatment of it?' Momentarily confused, Gallia lets him slip away before she has summoned the courage to ask him at least to kiss her, and is left ruefully regretting the omission:

> Perhaps he would have said no; but if he would have consented to be simple, surely he would not have minded kissing me just once! A woman always grants as much, and shines in doing it. It is looked on as a sacrifice on her part, and no one thinks the worse of her. (ch. 9)

Later she finds a man prepared to sacrifice a good deal more of his physical integrity to her than this; but in the meantime, like Gwen Waring, she has to work off her frustrations with long rides across country.

Those men who do readily consent to be simple are at first safely separated off in Paris, where they dabble in art and keep giggling mistresses. Later Mark Gurdon, who has clung to the fringes of this society without condoning its indulgences, returns to England and falls in love with Essex's sister Margaret, a model of feminine innocence and charm. These two upright and inarticulate examples of conformity are used to expose the idiocy of the innocent. Mark stumbles through a set speech of proposal, which Margaret receives with maidenly modesty, and then adds a further clause assuring her of his sexual purity, which she greets with blank incomprehension. Her refusal of him is plain enough, however, and soon afterwards Mark meets the mistress of one of his friends and forfeits the right to give similar assurances in future: 'Since his refusal by Margaret Essex, he had been fighting down a severe attack of passion; this night on which he came across Cara had sensually roused him'. Here the novel begins an unblinking analysis of the generally ignored muddle between sex and love. Mark, sensually satisfied by his mistress, begins to see charms in Gallia, who has been considerably perked up by extracting a couple of loveless kisses from Essex. These sexual entanglements are meticulously summarised:

> Nature has no regard for the fitness of things, and life arranges the most tasteless contrasts. For instance, it was far from agreeable of them both to make Gallia attract Mark with the light lit by Essex's kisses, and it was equally *outré* in them to send Mark to the arms of his mistress with his head filled with the thoughts of another woman. (ch. 21)

Even more *outré*, however, is Gallia's final solution to Essex's continuing indifference. She reads up on eugenics, and decides that an 'eminently rational' course for her to pursue would be to pioneer the field of deliberate breeding, selecting a mate with the right physical characteristics to enable her to produce exemplary specimens of offspring. She has, in a sense, found a career. Thus she looks Mark over with all the dispassionate expertise she might bring to the judgement of a new horse, and decides that he will do. First, though, she has to endure all the preliminaries of proposal and acceptance, and here, like Hadria, she feels with sudden alarm that there might exist some innate feminine quality which forces women into conventional sentiment. Having stated categorically that she would be ashamed of herself if she ever came to love Mark, she is disturbed when, romantically framed by honeysuckle and roses, he finally asks her to marry him and she feels the stirrings of sexual response. She resists valiantly, but with only partial success:

'I can't be myself. All the dead women in the world who have done identical things at such moments are coercing me, are pushing and constraining me to act as they did. And if I do, I shan't mean it – it won't be me, it will be them – all the women who have been loved and who have gone before. . . . Women are like members of an Alpine party – looped each to one long rope. Even I, who have no sentiment in me, my hands and arms would know perfectly how to clasp you.'

Mark shivered with sudden passion. . . . (ch. 28)

He gets no opportunity to act on it, though, for the lecture moves on from the literary and historical conventions of love to the question of innate sexuality:

'There is no primary instinct of love making. It is heredity. A trick of heredity. Hands, arms, and lips are born with the cunning of it, and whether one feels like it or not has little enough to do with it.'

Mark admired her the more for this fire, though it puzzled him. . . . (ch. 28)

His final deflation comes when she turns to him and remarks devastatingly: 'I forget – have you said you loved me?' But at the end of the novel we are left to assume that he recovers sufficiently to perform his part in breeding the children and helping Gallia in her mission of improving the race, and that she regains the unemotional efficiency which will bring the best results. Gallia is meant to epitomise the modern woman's dilemma. Trapped between her independent intelligence and a hopeless love, she finally escapes into cold, self-contained dedication to an ideal. It is not, and is not intended to be, a happy picture, but is presented as a sign of the times.

Though said by the *Athenaeum* to contain some 'scabrous scenes',[24] *Gallia* was on the whole sympathetically received. Reviewers were becoming accustomed to the New Woman fiction, and judged Gallia herself, despite being 'so terribly modern', to be a comparatively likable example of an easily recognised type. The novel appeared in the same month as *The Woman Who Did*, and these two really represented the climax of the New Woman fiction. Critics began to look back and take stock of what had been happening to the English novel under the onslaught of feminist writers. In a long article on *Gallia*, the *Saturday Review* noted the startling way in which 'aspiring woman has given the lead to plodding man'.[25] Citing *The Heavenly Twins, A Superfluous Woman* and *A Yellow Aster* as other examples, it asked rhetorically 'what male novelist would have treated with similar boldness the sexual problem, that unveiling and exposure of the deformed image of Priapus in the innermost recesses of the Temple of Marriage?' To what extent this boldness is desirable is a judgement the writer seems reluctant to make, but others were more forthright. Blanche Leppington, in an article dauntingly entitled 'Debrutalisation of Man', made it perfectly clear where her sympathies lay. The New Woman novel, she claimed, 'is helping to carry the pressure of the moral question into the sacred enclosures of marriage itself, from which all questioning has been too long excluded; and it is perhaps hardly too much to say that no service could well be greater than this'.[26] And on the other side, Janet Hogarth, also announcing her allegiance in the title 'Literary Degenerates', saw the century 'tottering to its close' under a towering burden of decadence to which the New Woman novels had added considerable weight. Her only comfort is that 'sex mania in art and literature can be but a passing phase, and possibly the modern heroine's admirable manner of expressing herself may outlast her repulsive qualities, to the exceeding great benefit of literature and of society'.[27]

Janet Hogarth was in a sense right to point out the *fin-de-siècle* aspects of these novels. While the very name of the New Woman naturally associated her with the dynamic radicalism of the nineties, the novels in which she appeared seem to go beyond the demands of realism in their emphasis on failure, despair and death. To be driven to suicidal depression or madness is almost an essential part of the experience; though ostensibly used to show how genuinely difficult it is to escape the established order, it is also, as in the poetry of the nineties, savoured for its own sake. None of these writers allow their heroines to feel themselves part of a wider movement; the New Woman fiction as a whole gives the impression that large numbers of women are struggling in determined solitude to achieve an end which, because they are alone against society, is pre-ordained to be unattainable. The 'morbid' label which was slapped onto so many of the novels was not always misplaced. Though often used merely to indicate immorality – as Grant Allen points out when he makes Herminia Barton, reading the damning reviews of her revolutionary novel, cheer herself up with the thought that 'to be called morbid by the *Spectator* is sufficient proof that you have hit at least the right tack in morals' – it could also be applied legitimately. 'Morbid pessimism, subdued or paroxysmal, is the dominant note . . . of the "new" fiction' and satisfies modern woman's 'craving for the literature of hysteria and decadence', wrote Stutfield,[28] and the fact that the New Woman novels, presenting feminist arguments under a pall of pessimism, sold in such vast quantities gives significant support to his view. To be a New Woman was, it seems, to be determinedly miserable.

By about 1896 the craving appears to have been largely sated, and a notable change occurred in the presentation of the New Woman in fiction. Though George Egerton continued doggedly to pick out the *Keynotes* theme she went on the whole unheard, and others, such as Iota, simply threw in the towel. 'Mercifully the day of passionate problems, equally nauseous and improbable, is passing over', said the *Athenaeum*,[29] reviewing her utterly innocuous little novel *A Quaker Grandmother*. Mona Caird and Ménie Muriel Dowie continued to turn out competent enough work, but also seemed to assume that the public had had enough of passionate problems. The New Woman figures in their later novels, but not as a polemical centre. The type had become an established part of the literary repetoire and could now be used in minor roles or treated, as in Ménie Muriel Dowie's *The Crook of the Bough*, with a steely objectivity far removed from the crusading zeal which had previously been mustered in her cause. Grant Allen once more marched to his hill-top with the rousingly entitled *A Splendid Sin* (in which the hero discovers, to his delight, that he is not in fact the child of his mother's alcoholic husband but the product of a torrid extra-marital affair) but then belatedly began to see the funny side himself. *Miss Cayley's Adventures* (1899) sends its New Woman heroine round the world, intrepidly recovering stolen diamonds, winning a trans-Alpine bicycle race against all-male competition, and shooting a tiger in India. When a male admirer has the misfortune to slip over a Swiss precipice she hauls him up herself, explaining her strength to her nervous companions with the nonchalant assurance 'I often stroked a four at Girton'. In fact the New Woman became something of a comic stereotype: in Mary Beaumont's *Two New Women* (1899) the heroines – one a doctor, the other a landscape gardener – sit around flexing their biceps ('Feel that arm!') and boasting of their prowess in swimming and hockey matches. To their doting male consorts they appear 'quite the newest women! So emancipated that emancipation is a matter of ancient history, and they say nothing about it'. The New Woman was, indeed, rapidly becoming old hat.

The fiction of Sex and the New Woman flourished only for a few turbulent years. Its significance to the historian of feminism is obvious enough; to the literary critic, though, it may appear a deservedly neglected by-way of popular ephemera, quirkily interesting but of no great importance. But these novels probably had a far greater effect on literature than on the position of women. Firstly, by joining with such relish in the new movement to liberate fiction, and doing so on the wave of a popular debate about the liberation of women, they broke through the constricting bounds of conventional reticence and helped clear a path for better novelists to tread relatively unmolested. And secondly they provide a necessary context in which to judge the sudden emergence of feminist propaganda in the works of writers whose claims to attention on literary merit are securely established.

3 Thomas Hardy: New Women for Old

'If we consider broadly and without prejudice the tone and scope of the book', wrote Robert Tyrrell in his review of *Jude the Obscure*, 'we cannot but class it with the fiction of Sex and New Woman, so rife of late.'[1] To the reader of Hardy's earlier novels nothing would have seemed less likely than that he should end his career in fiction pilloried in the press as a champion of modish feminism. While men had drooled freely over his 'irresistibly fascinating' heroines, women of whatever persuasion were always reputed to shrink from them with disgust. 'Oh, how I *hate* Thomas Hardy', scrawled an irascible feminine hand in a library copy of *The Return of the Native*. 'The unpopularity of Mr Hardy's novels among women is a curious phenomenon', observed Edmund Gosse. 'Even educated women approach him with hesitation and prejudice. . . . There is something in his conception of the feminine character which is not well received.'[2] In Edith Slater's succinctly damning phrase, Hardy's heroines were generally considered by female readers to be 'in the worst sense, men's women'.[3]

Nevertheless, Hardy's last three major novels clearly embody ideas of central interest to the New Woman. In *The Woodlanders* a great deal is said in favour of divorce and against the discriminatory marriage laws; *Tess of the D'Urbervilles* is a powerful indictment of the double moral standard; and even Hardy himself, who often went to almost mendacious lengths in his attempts to dissociate his novels from contemporary problems, was forced to concede that *Jude the Obscure* at least 'involves' the marriage question. While Grace and Tess both pre-date the New Woman of popular fiction, each at various points expresses views which would command the admiration of these later heroines. And the first readers of *Jude the Obscure* would have every excuse for immediately identifying Sue Bridehead, with her quivering nerves and anti-marriage sentiments, as a typical New Woman of the neurotic school. This apparent development towards a feminist position, coinciding nicely with the widespread discussion of similar views by other writers, might suggest that Hardy's portrayal of women changed significantly under the influence of public debate. This is partly true. Sue Bridehead bears more than a superficial resemblance to other fictional New Women, and Hardy's characteristically un-informative allusion to Tryphena Sparks in the Preface to the first edition of *Jude* ('some of the circumstances' of the novel were 'suggested by the death of a woman' in 1890) adds far less to an understanding of her character than does a reading of the New Woman novels. But in fact Hardy arrived at his portrayal of advanced womanhood by a very different route from that of the committed feminist writers. The areas of interest which led his novels to converge on the New Woman fiction were sexual morality in general, and a pervading cynicism about marriage. Neither of these need necessarily imply a specifically feminist approach: indeed in many of his novels Hardy's view of women, and his ideas about sex and marriage, seem to pull him uncomfortably in different directions.

Edith Slater certainly had a point in seeing the typical Hardy heroine as essentially a man's woman. The sort of adjectives applied to her with indulgent approval by male reviewers – 'instinctive', 'pagan', 'capricious', 'vagrant' – were not on the whole those which women, particularly New Women, would like to hear applied to themselves. Hardy's heroines 'are for disturbing the peace of man', wrote Havelock Ellis in 1883,[4] and the idea of women distracting men from their higher purposes is one which runs right through the novels up to the point where Jude's hypnotic recital of his classical masters – 'Euripides, Aristotle, Plato, Lucretius. . .' – is interrupted by the sharp slap against his ear of the pig's pizzle flung by Arabella. In the earlier novels we see, for example, Boldwood transformed by Bathsheba's careless whim in sending the valentine from a success-ful, self-contained farmer into an almost insanely jealous suitor and eventually a murderer, and in *Two on a Tower* the ambitious young astronomer Swithin St. Cleeve having his gaze pulled irresistibly from the stars to Viviette. Almost invariably the women are fickle. Hardy's novels are full of innocent young men with bleeding hearts – Stephen Smith, Christopher Julian, John Loveday, George Somerset – and honest countrymen like Gabriel Oak, Diggory Venn and Giles Winterborne plod sturdily in the path of their wayward young ladies. Ironies, sometimes incongruously sharp, are frequently levelled against men who trust too readily in a woman's integrity. At the end of *Under the Greenwood Tree* Dick, having finally persuaded Fancy Day to marry him, laboriously expands on his belief in her honesty:

> Why we are so happy is because there is such full confidence between us. Ever since that time you confessed to that little flirtation with Shiner by the river . . . I have thought how artless and good you must be to tell me o' such a trifling thing, and to be so frightened about it as you were. It has won me to tell you my every deed and word since then. We'll have no secrets from each other, darling, will we ever? – no secrets at all. (Part V, ch 2)

What he does not know is that a rather less trifling thing had occurred after the Shiner incident – Dick's frank little wife had, while supposedly engaged to him, actually accepted a proposal of marriage from the vicar. The novel ends with the flirtatious Fancy listening to the song of the nightingale – 'Tippiwit! swe-e-et! Ki-ki-ki! Come hither, come hither, come hither!' – and thinking 'of a secret she would never tell'. This characteristic of partial confession persists through many of the heroines up to Sue Bridehead, who touchingly confides to Phillotson that Jude has held her hand, but omits to mention that he has kissed her.

The fact that Hardy's women are typically seen as a hindrance to men, captivating yet essentially separate from the sterner demands of life, has the effect of actually heightening the differences between the sexes. This was a feature of his work which was noted with approval by the *New Quarterly Magazine*: 'Those who believe, with the present writer, that the old antithesis of "manly" and "womanly" covers an essential natural truth, will not quarrel with Mr Hardy for the exaggeration which is in the main a tribute to it'.[5] Actually, though, the deep divisions between men and women apparent in most of Hardy's novels are not at all based on conventional notions of the old antithesis. Indeed many attributes of Hardy's heroines are also those of New Women, but are put to very different use. For example, almost all his women have a good formal education or a quick native intelligence. It is not only Sue Bridehead who claims intellectual superiority over her lover: Fancy Day is a qualified schoolmistress who marries the tranter's son; Elfride Swancourt, with chilling tact, deliberately loses her games of chess with bumbling Stephen Smith; Bathsheba Everdene explains her reasons for not marrying Oak with 'luminous distinctness': 'I am better educated than you – and I don't love you a bit'; and when Grace Melbury returns home polished and refined by her boarding-school her old liaison with Giles seems incongruous and demeaning. The educational advantage that the women have over their men is often matched by a financial one. Hardy appears to have compensated for the rejection of his first novel by returning obsessively to the Poor Man and the Lady theme in later works. Thus Bathsheba Everdene and Paula Power are actually the employers of their future husbands; Elfride and Elizabeth-Jane fall in love with men employed by their fathers, and Viviette Constantine acts as Swithin's patroness, buying his affections with a new telescope. Apparently Hardy liked to feel that his men were after something rare and precious; the woman's attraction is enhanced by her remoteness, but if she herself places too high a premium on her superiority she is punished either by misery with her husband or the mortification of having to run after the spurned object – a sweet reward for the man.

Indeed Hardy's women do a lot of running. Bathsheba begins her relationship with Oak by panting after him to deliver the assurance that he is perfectly at liberty to love her so long as he does not expect a return, and concludes it by seeking him out in the hope that he will propose again. Paula trails miserably round Normandy in the footsteps of George Somerset, at one point pursuing him at top speed down a busy street only to see him dodge her onto a train. 'It isn't every man who gets a woman in my position to run after him on foot, and alone', exclaims Paula, with 'tears of vexation in her eyes'. These scenes are obviously contrived not, as they would be in a New Woman novel, to emphasise the equality in courtship between men and women, but to give the suffering man the heady satisfaction of having a highly desirable woman humiliate herself for his sake – this is, essentially, the point that Paula makes. On the other hand, physical strength or agility in women is also seen as attractive for its own sake. We first see Ethelberta, in the days before social graces have spoilt her, dashing madly across country in pursuit of a duck-hawk. On the morning of his first day in the Swancourt household Stephen looks out of his window to be greeted with the charming picture of Elfride 'without hat or bonnet, running with a boy's velocity' after a pet rabbit. Later she uses her prowess as a horsewoman both to fascinate and to assert her superiority. A dash of the tomboy often adds spice to the charm of Hardy's heroines.

Oak watches enthralled as Bathsheba, sitting astride instead of decorously side-saddle, lies acrobatically along her pony's back to avoid overhanging branches; later he hears how, on discovering her bailiff stealing grain, she 'fleed at him like a cat—never such a tomboy as she is'. In *A Laodicean* Dare pumps the servants for information about what Paula gets up to in her gymnasium, and having learnt that she 'wears such a pretty boy's costume, and is so charming in her movements, that you think she is a lovely youth and not a girl at all', lures De Stancy to a chink in the wall, plies him with brandy, and leaves him to enjoy the sight of Paula in the 'absolute abandonment to every muscular whim that could take possession of such a supple form'. 'To precisely describe Captain De Stancy's admiration', comments Hardy, wisely retreating into reticence, 'was impossible'.

The fact that Hardy's women are characteristically capricious, fickle and often childishly emotional seems to place them firmly on the side of convention; the advantage they hold over their suitors in terms of brains, wealth and physical skills inclines them in the opposite direction. The typical Hardy heroine will, as Mrs Swancourt says of her step-daughter, 'say things worthy of a French epigrammatist, and act like a robin in a green-house'. It is an extremely piquant mixture, but definitely one to tickle the taste of men rather than women. However, Hardy does allow many of his heroines a degree of independence which would make them more interesting to the reader with feminist leanings. In the early novels, Cytherea, Fancy, Bathsheba and Ethelberta all earn their own living, the first two admittedly by entirely acceptable means, but the others in a decidedly eccentric fashion. When Bathsheba takes over full management of the farm she has inherited she promises her men: 'I shall be up before you are awake; I shall be afield before you are up; and I shall have breakfast before you are afield. In short, I shall astonish you all'. And for a time, indeed, she does. Once Ethelberta has won fame and a degree of fortune in her rather odd profession of high society story-teller, she achieves an impressive level of emancipation. She stands, says Hardy,

as all women stand who have made themselves remarkable by their originality, or devotion to any singular cause, as a person freed of her hampering and inconvenient sex, and, by virtue of her popularity, unfettered from the conventionalities of manner prescribed by custom for household womankind. The charter to

move abroad unchaperoned, which society for good reasons
grants only to three sorts – the famous, the ministering, and the
improper – Ethelberta was in a fair way to make splendid use of:
instead of walking in protected lanes she experienced that luxury
of isolation which normally is enjoyed by men alone. (ch. 31)

It is true that both women's careers end when they marry, and
moreover are relinquished without regret. In fact, though their
work gives them additional originality, almost all Hardy's heroines
enjoy an unusual amount of independence before marriage. This is
largely because his novels show a very high parent mortality rate.
Cytherea, Bathsheba, Thomasin, Paula and Viviette are orphans;
Fancy, Elfride, Eustacia, Grace and Sue have one parent living,
though Sue never sees her father and only Grace really bends to
paternal influence. A young woman living a conventionally secure
home life is a rarity in Hardy's novels; when his heroines marry they
do so on the whole by their own, not their parents', choice. Thus if
marriages go wrong – and in Hardy's novels they usually do – the
responsibility is placed squarely with the participants, and since it is
generally the woman who has chosen unwisely from among several
possible suitors it is she who has to seek a solution. In the end this is
condensed by Sue Bridehead into forceful opposition to marriage as
an institution.

Of course, Hardy had personal reasons for feeling that marriage
did not invariably lead to a happy ending, and perhaps because of
this was always rather cautious about making his own views public
except when he could hide behind the screen of fiction. However,
when in 1894 the *New Review* asked him for his opinion on pre-
marital sex education for the Young Person he followed his statement in favour of 'a plain handbook on natural processes' with a
suggestion that the inquiry was anyway somewhat misdirected:

> As your problems are given on the old lines, so I take them, without
> entering into the general question whether marriage, as we at
> present understand it, is such a desirable goal for all women as it is
> assumed to be; or whether civilization can escape the humiliating
> indictment that . . . it has never succeeded in creating that
> homely thing, a satisfactory scheme for the conjunction of the
> sexes.[6]

And two years later he wrote sadly to Florence Henniker: 'Seriously,

I don't see any possible scheme for the union of the sexes that would be satisfactory'.[7] Neither comment approaches the heights of shrill denunciation found in the hard-liners of anti-marriage propaganda, but in his novels as well as in his personal writings Hardy habitually adopted for any observation on marriage a tone of weary despair rather than fighting fury. Cynical gibes at marriage gratuitously punctuate the novels: in *Far from the Madding Crowd* Hardy offers the opinion, apropos of very little, that 'there is no regular path for getting out of love as there is for getting in. Some people look upon marriage as a short cut that way, but it has been known to fail'. In *Two on a Tower*, as Viviette wanders round Bath waiting for Swithin to come and marry her, 'she appeared to be the single one of the human race bent upon marriage business, which seemed to have been unanimously abandoned by all the rest of the world as proven folly'. Elizabeth-Jane 'knew in spite of her maidenhood that marriage was as a rule no dancing matter', and the rustics, accustomed to delivering themselves of aphoristic insights, tend to wax grimly humorous at the sight of a newly wed couple: 'When folks are just married 'tis as well to look glad o't, since looking sorry won't unjoin 'em', says Timothy Fairway in *The Return of the Native*. And even the unusually mellow ending of *Far from the Madding Crowd*, with Bathsheba and Oak sitting peacefully at tea after their wedding, is given slightly sharper tones by the concluding dialogue of the sagacious countrymen:

> 'I never heerd a skilful old married feller of twenty years' standing pipe "my wife" in a more used note than 'a did,' said Jacob Smallbury. 'It might have been a little more true to nater if't had been spoke a little chillier, but that wasn't to be expected just now.'
> 'That improvement will come wi' time,' said Jan. (ch. 57)

The voice of homely experience pronouncing marriage to be a sure road to misery rises to an almost comic crescendo in *Jude the Obscure*, though it is balanced by the more rational, but by then fairly commonplace, arguments of Sue Bridehead.

Before Sue steps forward to carry the New Woman's anti-marriage banner there is little direct discussion of the institution in Hardy's novels. His view seems to be simply that it is deceptively easy for people to get married and disastrously difficult for them to untangle the knots of legal and social obligation that such a small ceremony ties them up in. The fact that Hardy's heroines are either largely unsupervised or entirely independent greatly facilitates their matrimonial misadventures, and there is scarcely a wedding in his work which is not secret, abortive or runaway. Because his women, despite their intelligence, are usually flighty and inconsistent, they have a built-in predilection for making the wrong choice. Although Troy and Wildeve both marry casually and without deep feeling it is more often the conventionally 'feminine' qualities in the heroines which prod an ill-matched couple to the altar. Thus Cytherea marries for financial support; Bathsheba is piqued into marrying Troy when he expresses admiration for another woman; Ethelberta shamelessly bargains for wealth and a title – ' "How lovely," said Ethelberta, as she looked at the fairy ascent. "His staircase alone is worth my hand!" ' Viviette, desperate for a husband to legitimise her child, lands a bishop in the nick of time; Thomasin marries because she would look foolish if she did not, and Sue hastens her wedding with Phillotson to punish Jude for not revealing the existence of Arabella. None of these marriages is successful, and each leaves an honest suitor lamenting his loss.

In at least two of his novels, Hardy had either to alter or tone down his original ending to make his view of love seem less bleak: *The Return of the Native* was to have left Thomasin a widow and Diggory Venn a lonely wanderer, and on *The Woodlanders* Hardy wrote to J. T. Grein:

> You have probably observed that the ending of the story – hinted rather than stated – is that the heroine is doomed to an unhappy life with an inconstant husband. I could not accentuate this strongly in the book, by reason of the conventions of the libraries, etc.[8]

Even when, as in *Far From the Madding Crowd*, he had planned a genuinely happy ending, his desire to reward the hero can be seen to tug uneasily against his conception of the woman. It is of course fitting that Bathsheba should finally have to make approaches to the long-suffering Oak, but her reasons for doing so are by no means as flattering as he might suppose. When Oak hands in his notice and announces his intention of emigrating, Bathsheba feels

aggrieved and wounded that the possession of hopeless love from Gabriel, which she had grown to regard as her inalienable right for life, should have been withdrawn just at his own pleasure in this way. She was bewildered too by the prospect of having to rely on her own resources again: it seemed to herself that she never could again acquire energy sufficient to go to market, barter, and sell. Since Troy's death Oak had attended all sales and fairs for her, transacting her business at the same time with his own. What should she do now? (ch. 56)

In other words, Oak's defection is personally humiliating and practically inconvenient, so Bathsheba dons her bonnet and cloak and goes off to indicate her willingness to let him marry her. The ensuing scene, with a tearful Bathsheba by turns coyly inviting and banteringly reproachful, is, of course, sufficiently touching, but almost as if he is afraid that the implications of its introduction are too disturbing Hardy follows it with a weighty lecture explaining why the two are genuinely well suited:

> Theirs was that substantial affection which arises . . . when the two who are thrown together begin first by knowing the rougher sides of each other's character, and not the best till further on, the romance growing up in the interstices of a mass of hard prosaic reality. This good-fellowship – *camaraderie* – usually occurring through similarity of pursuits, is unfortunately seldom super-added to love between the sexes, because men and women associate, not in their labours, but in their pleasures merely. Where, however, happy circumstance permits its development, the compounded feeling proves itself to be the only love which is strong as death. (ch. 56)

It is hard to see how the two passages can fuse into a coherent image.

Anti-marriage sentiments, of whatever flavour, would obviously pull Hardy some way towards the New Woman novels, even though the rather disproportionate responsibility assigned to women for the matrimonial messes with which the novels are strewn would hardly please the feminists. However, Hardy is a good deal more sympathetic towards women in his treatment of sex. His heroines may be condemned for the careless exercise of sexual power which enslaves worthy men, but in deeper relationships, or if seduced and betrayed, they always have his full support. Hardy had no patience with traditional demands for purity in women, and with *Tess of the D'Urbervilles* he got himself into serious trouble for saying so. In fact he was always pushing his readers to the limits of their tolerance about sexual matters. *Desperate Remedies* had to be altered to cut out reference to 'the violation of a young lady at an evening party' (the published version revealed merely that 'a young girl of seventeen was cruelly betrayed by her cousin') and to make it less obvious that Manston's false wife was also his mistress. *Far from the Madding Crowd* brought Hardy a shower of personal correspondence objecting to the staining of its rural purity by Fanny Robin and her illegitimate child, and *Two on a Tower*, in which Viviette is seen stealing from her home at night to visit Swithin's bed, brought down a torrent of the *Spectator*'s epithets of moral outrage – the story was 'unpleasant' 'objectionable' and 'repulsive'.[9] But it was in *The Woodlanders, Tess* and *Jude* that Hardy directed his views on sex and marriage towards themes which for contemporary readers clearly associated him with current feminist debates.

The 1895 Preface to *The Woodlanders* is interesting for the remarkably clumsy way in which Hardy attempts both to defend himself and to wriggle out of making any explicit statements about the views on marriage expressed in the novel. For the writer who wished to maintain a reputation as a serious artist rather than a propagandist for fashionable ideas, 1895 was not, of course, a good year for coming out with unequivocal anti-marriage pronounce-ments, but even so Hardy's havering seems both inept and somewhat cowardly. 'In the present novel', he writes, '. . . the immortal puzzle – given the man and woman, how to find a basis for their sexual relation – is left where it stood; and it is tacitly assumed for the purposes of the story that no doubt of the depravity of the erratic heart who feels some second person to be better suited to his or her tastes than the one with whom he has contracted to live, enters the head of reader or writer for a moment.' The ironic tone seems to be aimed at the wrong target. In claiming that no such doubt has entered the writer's head, Hardy is quite unnecessarily convicting himself of having written an extremely bad novel: nobody could for a moment interpret Grace as depraved in her cooling towards Fitzpiers, and in any case, were it not for the moral inequality in the divorce laws which makes it impossible for her to dissolve her marriage on the grounds of her husband's adultery, a perfectly satisfactory basis for the relationship of Grace and Giles could have been found. Hardy continues with a virtual con-tradiction of his previous statement:

From the point of view of marriage as a distinct covenant or undertaking, decided on by two people fully cognizant of all its possible issues, and competent to carry them through, this assumption is, of course, logical. Yet no thinking person supposes that, on the broader ground of how to afford the greatest happiness to the units of human society during their brief transit through this sorry world, there is no more to be said on this covenant; and it is certainly not supposed by the writer of these pages.

He concludes this sorry muddle with a quotation: 'as Gibbon blandly remarks on the evidence for and against Christian miracles, "the duty of an historian does not call upon him to interpose his private judgement in this nice and important controversy"'. Hardy's use of the word 'blandly' suggests that he was perfectly aware that Gibbon is as sceptical about Christian miracles in *The Decline and Fall* as Hardy is about the sanctity of marriage in *The Woodlanders* and *Jude*. Indeed, exactly the same device of dissemblance through pretended objectivity is used in *Jude the Obscure*. In a letter to Gosse, Hardy claimed that 'the only remarks which can be said to bear on the *general* marriage question occur in dialogue. . . . And of these remarks I state . . . that my own views are not expressed therein'.[10] The statement he refers to is in fact nothing more than a slight rewording of the passage from Gibbon: 'The purpose of a chronicler of moods and deeds does not require him to express his personal views on the grave controversy above given'. Hardy's own position is always more clear than he liked to pretend; only with *Tess of the D'Urbervilles* was he always prepared to stand firmly by what he had written.

   Although *The Woodlanders* is a great deal more than a mere tract on divorce, the miraculous appearance of the 'new law' and its subsequently revealed shortcomings are important both for the plot and in the development of Grace's emotions. F. B. Pinion in *A Hardy Companion* states that 'the new divorce law of 1878 and Hardy's reference in 1926 to the period of the novel ("fifty years ago" . . .) leave no doubt that the story extends from 1876 to 1879'.[11] On the face of it this seems a little odd. The first page of the novel describes the time as 'a bygone winter's day' – a curious way of referring to a date eleven years before publication; nor does Hardy specifically refer to the period of the novel as 'fifty years ago' – he merely says in answer to a question about the real location of Little Hintock that it

'has features which were to be found fifty years ago' in various
Dorset villages. Anyway Hardy's researches were more thorough
than Mr Pinion's: the shady lawyer who tells Melbury about the
new statute actually quotes its number – it is 'twenty and twenty-
one Vic., cap. eighty-five', the Matrimonial Causes Act of 1857.
The novel is thus set at a date when the mere thought of divorce
seemed startlingly modern, and shows the way in which the law at
first fosters desirable moral developments and then crushes the
budding freedom into disastrous conformity.[12]

It is not only in the backwoods of Little Hintock that divorce
seems an entirely new concept. The sophisticated Fitzpiers is
surprised and shocked when he hears that Grace has sought legal
redress; Hardy allows that the lawyer, though perhaps guilty of
deliberate duplicity, is probably also honestly ignorant of the act's
exact provisions. Even so, Hardy makes the naivety of such a
deserving couple as Grace and Giles seem particularly poignant in
contrast to the rigour and complexity of the law. 'Have you to sign a
paper, or swear or anything?' Grace asks, and to a readership who
by 1887 would be thoroughly familiar with newspaper accounts of
the sensational and often sordid transactions of the divorce courts
the irony of such a question would be obvious. 'To hear these two
Arcadian innocents talk of imperial law would have made a
humane person weep', comments Hardy. It is not merely that the
law fails to furnish simple remedies, though. More importantly, it
does not coincide with mature moral sense. Long before they hear of
the miraculous appearance of the new law, both Grace and her
father have been brought by experience to a reassessment of their
earlier moral assumptions. When Grace hears the truth about Suke
Damson's relationship with Fitzpiers she

> was almost startled to find how little she suffered from that jealous
> excitement which is conventionally attributed to all wives in such
> circumstances. But though possessed by none of the feline
> wildness which it was her moral duty to experience, she did not
> fail to suspect that she had made a frightful mistake in her
> marriage. Aquiescence in her father's wishes had been de-
> gradation to herself. (ch. 29)

And at almost the same time, Melbury begins to question his
previous unthinking conformity: 'He knew that a woman once
given to a man for life took, as a rule, her lot as it came, and made

the best of it, without external interference; but for the first time he asked himself why this so generally should be done'. Grace's love for Giles reawakens before she has any reason to hope that it may be legally fulfilled in marriage; when Fitzpiers thinks she is sulking at the breakfast table as a result of his petulant moans about marriage she is in fact quiet only because she is mentally rehearsing the sterling qualities of her old lover. She is almost as unfaithful in thought as he is in deed.

So when the new law appears as a 'mysterious, beneficent, god-like entity' it seems to Grace not something which will suddenly shake her out of her old convictions about the sanctity of marriage but a convenient way of regularising a situation which her developing moral awareness has already approved. For a short time she is allowed to believe that the law endorses her independent judgement. Although in her meetings with Giles she does not permit many physical freedoms it is, as she tells him, her sense of social propriety that holds her back, 'not that I feel bound to any one else after what has taken place – no woman of spirit could'. When Melbury returns bitterly enlightened about legal realities – 'I was deluded. He has not done you *enough* harm!' – Grace has gone too far in moral emancipation to accept the law's interpretation of her duty. Though her father, always one false step ahead of his daughter's wishes, advises Grace to make the best of things with Fitzpiers, she sets off to seek Giles's help in running away. Here her progression towards liberty with the conventions has to be slowed down in order to keep Giles out in the rain long enough to cause his death. She stands out on a moral quibble:

> You know what I feel for you – what I have felt for no other living man, what I shall never feel for a man again. But as I have vowed myself to somebody else than you, and cannot be released, I must behave as I do behave, and keep that vow. I am not bound to him by any divine law, after what he has done; but I have promised, and I will pay. (ch. 41)

Quite how it would be breaking her vow to Fitzpiers to let a sick man sleep in the same room with her – Giles's intentions are strictly honourable, and in any case he is too ill to be anything else – is not clear. But when she relents, she does so emphatically, and perhaps with an invitation to more than a dry shelter: '*Come to me, dearest! I don't mind what they say or what they think of us any more*'. His cool response – 'It is not necessary for me to come' – shows him a willing martyr to the proprieties, but after his death Grace exults in allowing Fitzpiers to draw 'the extremest inference' from her stay in Giles's home and feels 'a thrill of pride' in her daring. Ironically, when she reaches her highest point of rebellion against conventional morality, she brings herself at last under the provisions of the law; despite the fact that she is lying, the evidence and her confession are so much against her that Fitzpiers would have no difficulty in obtaining a divorce.

After this Grace sinks steadily towards conformity. She even rereads the marriage service and wonders 'whether God really did join them together'. In her return to Fitzpiers she shows the same sort of docility under strong influence which had led her to marry him in the first place, and though Hardy could not go as far as he wished in establishing her future unhappiness, Melbury's final reflections seem fairly conclusive:

> Well – he's her husband . . . and let her take him back to her bed if she will! . . . But let her bear in mind that the woman walks and laughs somewhere at this very moment whose neck he'll be coling next year as he does hers to-night. . . . It's a forlorn hope for her; and God knows how it will end! (ch. 48)

Although Hardy says little in his own voice about the morality of divorce it is perfectly clear which way the reader's sympathies are directed. The law which would apparently bring deserved relief from misery turns out to be patently unjust and inadequate. Hardy certainly does not support the moral judgement implied by the law's double standard, that adultery in a man is insignificant, something almost to be expected. Fitzpiers, the confirmed sensualist, can only be condemned by comparison with the sturdy Giles. Indeed Fitzpiers takes quite an authorial lashing:

> The love of men like Fitzpiers is unquestionably of such quality as to bear division and transference. He had indeed once declared . . . that on one occasion he had noticed himself to be possessed by five distinct infatuations at the same time. If this were true, his differed from the highest affection as the lower orders of the animal world differ from advanced organisms, partition causing not death but a multiplied existence. (ch. 29)

His attitude towards Grace's supposed adultery is also interesting. Unlike Angel Clare, he is not condemned for a blindly hypocritical adherence to the double moral standard; instead he actually goes one better and creates a sort of treble standard reflecting his own peculiar blend of the sensual with the conformist. He is 'stung into passionate throbs of interest' when he believes that his meek little wife has been unfaithful; 'melancholy as it may be to admit the fact', says Hardy, Grace's misconduct has 'engendered a smouldering admiration' in him. He is more aroused than appalled by her behaviour, but far from taking this as a basis for reconciliation, he refrains from making his repentant approaches until he has heard from Marty South that Grace is pure after all. For Fitzpiers Grace is either an adulteress, fascinating but no longer suitable as a wife, or a wronged innocent, easily lured back to the matrimonial fold, who can be betrayed without fear of sexual reprisal in the future. The poor girl cannot win.

Divorce in *The Woodlanders* is of central importance for the plot. If the law had reflected what the novel shows to be moral justice Giles would not have died and Grace could have been happy in a second marriage. But the very fact that all the characters are prepared to abide finally by both the law and the proprieties makes the novel essentially less challenging in its social theme than those which followed it. In *Tess* and *Jude* Hardy is more concerned with establishing a sexual morality which can stand out against both legal and social demands. Tess regrets that she is unable legally to give Angel Clare his freedom, but the reader feels that he has no adequate reason for wanting it; Jude and Sue get their divorces through the post – both are granted on the grounds of wife's adultery, and so are perfectly straightforward – but this is no help to them in establishing a basis for their relationship. Like the New Woman writers, Hardy shows himself to be in favour of freer divorce, but by no means confident that a fairly minor adjustment of the law would sweep away all the problems of sex and marriage in the modern world.

Tess of the D'Urbervilles and *Jude the Obscure*, the novels which brought Hardy into the centre of contemporary controversy, both have clear precedents in his own work. He had used similar themes and characters in other novels, but in the freer atmosphere of the nineties and, particularly with *Jude*, under the influence of the popular enthusiasm for the New Woman question, he brought his earlier interests into sharper, and perhaps more fashionable, focus.

In the 1912 Preface to *A Pair of Blue Eyes*, Hardy says that the novel 'exhibits the romantic stage of an idea which was further developed in a later book'. This gratuitous offering of information while withholding the vital facts is, regrettably, typical of Hardy, but there seems little doubt that the further developments he refers to come in *Tess of the D'Urbervilles*. In both novels the heroine loses the man she loves when a damaging secret about her sexual past is revealed, and in both cases the man is shown to be ludicrously unjust in his inflexible demand for purity in a woman. Of course, *A Pair of Blue Eyes* is still very much in the 'romantic stage' – Elfride, despite her country ways and tomboyish wildness, is essentially a society girl, and her flirtations are the innocent experiments of a youthful heart – but thematically much of the novel looks like an early and necessarily more circumspect sketch for *Tess*.

For example, Elfride combines the typical attributes of the Hardy heroine – mature intelligence, infantile emotionalism, capriciousness, inconstancy and so on – with a more unusual sensuality which provokes much gloating from both characters and author. Like Tess, she carries with her an unconsciously seductive manner which enslaves men whether she wants it or not. Tess is at her most attractive when working in the fields, and Elfride, also an outdoor girl, is constantly having the outlines of her body emphasised by the wind. Stephen watches fascinated as she 'went away into the wind . . . in which gust she had the motions, without the motives, of a hoyden; the grace, without the self-consciousness, of a pirouetter'. Later Knight sees her in a similarly captivating scene: 'The ends of her hanging hair softly dragged themselves backwards and forwards upon her shoulder as each faint breeze thrust against or relinquished it. Fringes and ribbons of her dress, moved by the same breeze, licked like tongues upon the parts around them'. Here it is the language which is overtly sensual; in the scene where Elfride strips to the skin to make a rope from her clothes with which to haul Knight up the cliff, the whole situation is extremely erotic. Admittedly she replaces her outer garments, but as she is soaked by the rain and buffeted by the wind they do not do much to disguise her semi-nudity; even Knight, with his life hanging almost literally by a thread, cannot help noticing how her clothes 'seemed to cling to her like a glove'. After his rescue, while there is still nothing between him and her naked body but a 'diaphanous exterior robe', he embraces her lingeringly – it is hardly surprising that despite being 'wet and chilled' he is 'glowing with fervour nevertheless'.

More important, though, is the treatment of the fallen woman theme. At first, of course, it never enters Knight's head that any accusation of sexual impurity could be levelled against Elfride; what concerns him is the possibility that she should have so much as looked at a man before him. Like Angel Clare, he demands perfect 'freshness' in the woman he marries, and when he discovers that she has loved another man he too feels most unreasonably that she is some sort of impostor. Both men fall in love with a moral quality rather than a woman, and when Elfride realises this she stands up for herself quite impressively:

> Am I such a – mere characterless toy – as to have no attraction in me, apart from – freshness? Haven't I brains? You said – I was clever and ingenious in my thoughts, and – isn't that anything? Have I not some beauty? . . . You have praised my voice, and my manner, and my accomplishments. Yet all these things together are so much rubbish because I – accidentally saw a man before you! (ch. 32)

At this point Knight's absurd scruples derive more from the peculiar nature of his individual preference than from a prevailing moral attitude, though Hardy does indicate the irony of his wish that he had had more sexual experience and Elfride less. But when he learns about Elfride's overnight escapade with Stephen Smith he leaps to the conclusion that she is a fallen woman and begins to react as a representative of social morality. His reflections typify the muddled thinking of a conventional man who has discovered unpalatable facts about the sexual experience of the woman he loves:

> Elfride loved him, he knew, and he could not leave off loving her; but marry her he would not. If she could but be again his own Elfride – the woman she had seemed to be – but that woman was dead and buried, and he knew her no more! And how could he marry this Elfride, one who, if he had originally seen her as she was, would have been barely an interesting pitiable acquaintance in his eyes – no more? (ch. 35)

Of course Knight is, as it happens, wrong about Elfride – her one night alone with Stephen had been spent quite chastely in the London to Plymouth express – but his ideas on female purity have by this time been so thoroughly discredited that even when he moves from a merely personal to a generally accepted moral stance it is impossible not to condemn him. Both *A Pair of Blue Eyes* and *Tess of the D'Urbervilles* make intelligent polemical use of the device of discovery: if a woman appears to be one sort of character, can the revelation of a single past action really make her into something utterly different? Hardy's answer in both cases is no, but whereas in the earlier novel the question is largely theoretical, in *Tess* the argument can be backed up by evidence from the action.

Tess herself is unique among Hardy's heroines in being quite clearly the victim of men's cruelty. As we have seen, the usual pattern is for men to suffer as a result of woman's caprice; Tess alone unquestionably experiences more misery than she inflicts. She is also untypical in her integrity. It is most unusual to find one of Hardy's heroines standing out against the generality of feminine behaviour as Tess does when Alec D'Urberville sneeringly retorts to her excuse that she had not understood his meaning till it was too late, 'that's what every woman says': 'My God! I could knock you out of the gig!' exclaims Tess, 'Did it never strike your mind that what every woman says some women may feel?' Also, unlike Hardy's other women, she remains honest when dissemblance would be greatly to her advantage. Her silly, simple mother sends Tess away to a fate at which she can guess shrewdly enough with the thought 'If he don't marry her afore he will after' and when her daughter returns home pregnant and unmarried is disappointed and angry: 'And yet th'st not got him to marry 'ee! . . . Any woman would have done it but you, after that!' Tess's refusal to scheme in the tacitly accepted way does not derive from unsophisticated innocence – her rejection of the best practical course is informed and deliberate, as she tells D'Urberville:

> I have never really and truly loved you, and I think I never can. . . . Perhaps of all things, a lie on this thing would do the most good to me now; but I have honour enough left, little as 'tis, not to tell that lie. If I did love you I may have the best o' causes for letting you know it. But I don't. (ch. 12)

By sacrificing her own interest to honesty, and doing so in a context where women would normally be expected – indeed encouraged – to do the opposite, Tess is unwittingly making a more general protest for women against the social conventions which foster deceit as an essential part of their nature. Hardy's usual depiction of women entrapping men is here entirely reversed, and sympathy is moved over wholesale to the woman.

These features of Tess's characterisation are necessary for the novel's argument. Hardy's hesitant approaches towards a similar theme in *A Pair of Blue Eyes*, even allowing for its abstract and circumlocutory treatment, could not have anything like the same polemical strength because the heroine is essentially infirm, prevaricating and, as Hardy saw it, typically feminine in her damaging desire to charm. In *Tess of the D'Urbervilles* Hardy is arguing unequivocally in support of the fallen woman, and his characterisation of the heroine is adjusted in order to remove all possibility of irrelevant criticism: objections to Tess can only be on the grounds of her sexual behaviour and must therefore derive from what Hardy attempts to show is a false morality. Testimony to the clarity of his purpose is given in the uncharacteristically forceful arguments of his prefaces to the novel. For the only time, he went on the offensive at once and stuck manfully to his guns. In the Preface to the first edition, he wrote:

> In respect of the book's opinions and sentiments, I would ask any too genteel reader, who cannot endure to have said what everybody nowadays thinks and feels, to remember a well-worn sentence of St. Jerome's: If an offence come out of the truth, better is it that the offence come than that the truth be concealed.

It is unusual enough to find Hardy conceding that a novel of his should embody opinions of any kind; to see him defending them so violently, as he does again in the 1892 Preface, is a unique experience. Here he positively snarls at his critics, expanding generously on his definition of the word 'pure' as used in the sub-title, and even inviting the judgement that he is deliberately and daringly pushing the treatment of the fallen woman theme into forbidden territory: 'This novel being one wherein the great campaign of the heroine begins after an event in her experience which has usually been treated as fatal to her part as protagonist, or at least as the virtual ending of her enterprises and hopes, it was quite contrary to avowed conventions that the public should welcome the book, and agree with me in holding that there was something more to be said in fiction than had been said about the shaded side of a well-known catastrophe.' Hardy is for once quite frank about embodying a recognisable contemporary 'problem' in his novel, and both his authorial comments and the structuring of the double-standard theme reveal a consistency and strength of purpose which leave no doubt that he is arguing undisguisedly in favour of an unpopular position.

From the beginning, Hardy stresses the sensuality of Tess's beauty – 'there was nothing ethereal about it; all was real vitality, real warmth, real incarnation' – and her affair with D'Urberville is seen as the natural, though unhappily ill-chosen, realisation of it. Though he slides over the period of their first liaison, we know that what began in September ends in late October, and Hardy shrugs off what might otherwise appear merely prudent reticence with a pointed dismissal of the incident's importance:

> She had dreaded him, winced before him, succumbed to adroit advantages he took of her helplessness; then, temporarily blinded by his ardent manners, had been stirred to confused surrender awhile: had suddenly despised and disliked him, and had run away. That was all. (ch. 12)

His 'that was all' is surely used not, as F. B. Pinion suggests,[13] to indicate that all D'Urberville had done after the initial seduction was passionately to proffer little presents, but, taken in conjunction with the laconic listing of events, to emphasise that Tess's affair follows a familiar and commonplace sequence and should provoke neither surprise nor outrage. Like Ruth, Tess feels that she has sinned, but unlike Mrs Gaskell, Hardy forces a complete dissociation between the heroine's judgement and the author's. When, on her flight from Trantridge, Tess encounters the itinerant painter of religious slogans, his words strike her with 'accusatory horror'; but Hardy, describing the 'staring vermilion words' standing out against the 'peaceful landscape', sees them as a 'hideous defacement – the last grotesque phase of a creed which had served mankind well in its time'. And later, as Tess thinks of herself as a scarlet woman clashing against the harmonious purity of nature, Hardy steps in peremptorily to contradict her:

> This encompassment of her own characterisation, based on shreds of convention, peopled by phantoms and voices antipathetic to her, was a sorry and mistaken creation of Tess's fancy – a cloud of moral hobgoblins by which she was terrified without reason. It was they that were out of harmony

with the actual world, not she. Walking among the sleeping birds
in the hedges, watching the skipping rabbits on a moonlit warren,
or standing under a pheasant-laden bough, she looked upon
herself as a figure of Guilt intruding into the haunts of Innocence.
But all the while she was making a distinction where there was no
difference. Feeling herself in antagonism she was quite in accord.
She had been made to break an accepted social law, but no law
known to the environment in which she fancied herself such an
anomaly. (ch. 13)

So when Angel Clare sees Tess as a 'fresh and virginal daughter of
Nature' he is, though ironically mistaken in his own terms, very
close to the truth in Hardy's. Tess is 'virginal' in the same sense that
she is 'pure', both terms being used to denote moral rather than
physical innocence. Clare, who, like Knight, is a self-consciously
modern thinker, showing 'considerable indifference to social forms
and observances', conclusively fails the first major test of his
emancipation and shows himself to be deeply entrenched in
convention in his attitude to women. In fact he is built up into an
even more monstrous figure than Knight. Hardy does not merely
argue the general unfairness of the double moral standard: he so
constructs the circumstances of Clare's sexual past and the movement towards the twin confession on the wedding night as to make
Angel seem positively diabolic in his injustice. His affair with the
woman in London is obviously a parallel to Tess's relationship with
D'Urberville – both are away from home, both are the victims of
partners older and presumably more experienced than themselves,
and both disengage themselves without emotional regret once the
infatuation wears off. Clare, we are told, 'was carried off his head,
and nearly entrapped by a woman much older than himself, though
luckily he escaped not greatly the worse for the experience'. With
Tess's affair, Hardy has to strive to emphasise its relative un-
importance; in Angel's case, because he is a man, the triviality is
obvious, but the situation is much the same. And when on his
wedding night Clare lightly and almost humorously confesses his
little peccadillo, his tale of hesitation and self-interest in concealing
the truth is almost identical to Tess's:

I did not mention it because I was afraid of endangering my
chance of you, darling. . . . I was going to tell you a month ago –
at the time you agreed to be mine, but I could not; I thought it

might frighten you away from me. I put it off; then I thought I would tell you yesterday, to give you a chance at least of escaping me. But I did not. And I did not this morning, when you proposed our confessing our faults on the landing – the sinner that I was! (ch. 34)

This is almost point for point the sequence of Tess's own attempts to confess. On the first occasion, just before she accepts his proposal, she draws back because 'her instinct of self-preservation was stronger than her candour', just as Angel admits to doing so because it might frighten her away; on the last, the morning of the wedding, she suggests that he should listen to an account of 'all my faults and blunders' and, with his own confession in his mind, he cuts her short – 'they will be excellent matter for a dull day'; and in between she goes further than he and actually writes the full account of her affair in the letter which fate conveniently shuffles under the carpet. Of course, Tess forgives Angel as he fully expects to be forgiven. But when he learns that her previous experience and conduct during their courtship is, in all essentials, exactly the same as his, he responds to her plea to 'forgive me as you are forgiven' with the chilling pronouncement 'forgiveness does not apply to the case! You were one person, now you are another'. The breathtaking injustice of his behaviour has the effect not primarily of arousing pity for Tess but of stirring rage and indignation against Clare. Here it is not so much that the fallen woman is treated as an object of compassion rather than disgust, but that an aggressive attack is mounted against the man and the social attitudes he represents.

This concentration on the man as the guilty figure is maintained throughout the scenes following Tess's confession. Clare is caught in a complex net of his own hypocrisy extending outwards from his adherence to the double moral standard through his accusation that Tess is 'a species of impostor; a guilty woman in the guise of an innocent one' to his whole attitude towards her as aristocratic peasant. Having at first regarded with complacency the blow he strikes at convention by loving a woman far beneath him in social status, he then displays a suspicious enthusiasm for her D'Urberville ancestry, and after her confession flings both aspects of her birth in her face. 'You almost make me say you are an uncomprehending peasant woman, who have never been initiated into the proportions of social things' he sneers, taunting her for timidly suggesting that some men may not mind about her past as much as he does. And when she defends herself by pathetically reminding him of the lineage over which he had previously gloated, he attributes her fall to the decrepit will of a decrepit family: 'Why did you give me a handle for despising you more by informing me of your descent! Here was I thinking you a new-sprung child of nature; there were you, the belated seedling of an effete aristocracy!'. Like Elfride, Tess tries to stand on her claims as an individual – 'I thought, Angel, that you loved me – me, my very self!' – but Clare too maintains that sexual conduct defines the woman. Later, however, Hardy allows Clare to creep back towards sympathy, as he retracts his offer to Izz Huett when he hears how much Tess loves him, and Tess herself becomes more obviously the innocent victim. There is still a faint residue of the idea found at its crudest in Mrs Gaskell that the fallen woman's claims to compassion must derive from exceptional personal qualities and not from objective justice. Tess's 'meekness', 'long-suffering' and 'endurance' in her love for Clare and her declaration that 'the punishment you have measured out to me is deserved . . . and you are quite right and just to be angry with me' tug pitifully at the emotions, even though the reader is persuaded that her judgement is wrong and Clare is unworthy of her love. Her misery is acute enough to pierce the stoniest moral heart. On the other hand, she does not remain the purely tragic sufferer: she returns to D'Urberville, and in her last letter to Clare finally turns on him:

> O why have you treated me so monstrously, Angel! I have thought it all over carefully, and I can never, never forgive you! You know that I did not intend to wrong you – why have you so wronged me? You are cruel, cruel indeed! I will try to forget you. It is all injustice I have received at your hands! (ch. 53)

'It is quite true', says Clare, confirming the reader's opinion.

Hardy's treatment of the fallen woman theme in *Tess* interestingly combines traditional features of proving the heroine's penitence through the meek endurance of misery with authorial commentary denying both the necessity and justice of such trials. He artfully gets the best of both worlds; the conventionally-minded reader is pushed towards sympathy for Tess because she suffers so beautifully, but the actual argument of the novel is directed more against the moral rigidity of the man and society. In the end, Tess herself realises that she was mistaken in accepting Clare's estimate of her, and by rebelling against her allotted literary role perhaps loses some of the sentimental sympathy to be expected from the contemporary reader. (Mrs Oliphant for one gave it as her opinion that 'according to any natural interpretation' Tess 'must have died of shame rather than meet the eyes of her husband clothed in the embroideries of the nightgown'.[14]) And although the fallen woman is still apparently condemned to premature death, Tess dies through the due processes of law for a murder she has really committed, not for some trumped-up demand that the sinner should purge her guilt by dying in tender self-sacrifice.

Tess of the D'Urbervilles appeared to its first readers as not only the most strongly argued of Hardy's novels, but also the most outspoken in its treatment of sexuality. It came to a public already jittery about the undermining of morals by French and Norwegian writers, but one not yet familiar with the ways in which this licence could be harnessed to the feminist bandwagon. Tess is not a New Woman, but the novel which is built around her embodies essential features of the New Woman fiction which followed it – disrespect for polite reticence about sex, combined with the presentation of a case in favour of some aspect of woman's emancipation. In calling Tess a 'pure woman' Hardy was aggressively advertising his polemical intention; like Grant Allen, he uses the word 'pure' in the exact opposite of its conventional meaning, and challenges his readers to disagree. Most of them did. Though fulsomely praised by some reviewers, the novel was treated by its many detractors in much the same way as the New Woman fiction; it was seen as dangerous in its ideas, 'coarse' and 'disagreeable' in its expression of them.

Tess immediately preceded the New Woman fiction; *Jude the Obscure* appeared at the point of its highest popularity. In *The Woodlanders* and *Tess* Hardy was discussing ideas of contemporary interest, particularly to feminists, and as we have seen his earlier work revealed a consistent if peripheral cynicism about marriage. It is scarcely surprising then that he should have joined in the general flurry of feminism and anti-marriage fervour of the time and produced a novel in which his earlier views on marriage are projected onto the then fashionable figure of a New Woman heroine. The novel was widely received as an addition to the New Woman fiction, and Sue Bridehead emerges as a curious hybrid, part contemporary feminist, and part the traditional Hardy heroine.

Sue has many of the characteristics already noted as common to the earlier heroines, but the most obvious precedent for her particular combination of modern independence with traditional feminine coquetry comes in *A Laodicean* with Paula Power. Paula, whose very name proclaims her almost masculine self-reliance, is 'emphatically a modern type of maidenhood'. She 'holds advanced views on social and other matters; and in those on the higher education of women she is very strong'; her antics in the gymnasium display her enthusiasm for 'this subject of the physical development of her sex'; and her eclectic reading is shown by the books which cram her room – novels in French and Italian and 'most of the popular papers and periodicals . . . not only English, but from Paris, Italy and America'. Like Sue in Christminster, Paula in her crumbling castle is 'a modern flower in a medieval flower-pot', and both women reject the medieval in favour of the classical: 'I am not a medievalist myself . . . I am Greek', says Paula, and Sue declares 'I am more ancient than medievalism'. Both George and Jude agonise over their lover's tantalising manner and wonder ruefully whether it is the product of deliberately contrived feminine wiles. 'Sue, I sometimes think you are a flirt', says Jude, and George, 'with a pang at his heart', suddenly perceives Paula as 'possibly a finished coquette and dissembler'. Paula's 'saucy independence', 'saucy composure' and 'gentle sauciness' blend with her self-conscious modernity and emancipation to produce for George a mix as maddening and delightful as Sue is for Jude, and in the end Paula mockingly defines herself in her union with George as 'a perfect representative of "the modern spirit"'.

But the modernity of 1881 is very different from that of 1895, and Sue Bridehead, though taking many of her characteristics specifically from Paula and generally from the earlier heroines, has also the distinctly contemporary features of the New Woman. In the 1912 Preface to *Jude* Hardy includes a lengthy passage on Sue as the modern feminist:

After the issue of *Jude the Obscure* as a serial story in Germany, an experienced reviewer of that country informed the writer that Sue Bridehead . . . was the first delineation in fiction of the woman who was coming into notice in her thousands every year – the woman of the feminist movement – the slight, pale 'bachelor' girl – the intellectualised, emancipated bundle of nerves that modern conditions were producing, mainly in cities as yet; who does not recognise the necessity for most of her sex to follow marriage as a profession, and boast themselves as superior people because they are licensed to be loved on the premises. The regret of this critic was that the portrait of the newcomer had been left to be drawn by a man, and was not done by one of her own sex, who would never have allowed her to break down at the end.

Whether this assurance is borne out by dates I cannot say. . . .

He certainly should have been able to say, and moreover to say quite definitely, that Sue was closer to being the last than the first delineation in fiction of this type. There is no reason why a German reviewer, however experienced, should have been aware of the New Woman fiction, but for an English novelist to profess ignorance of such a widely discussed movement is scarcely plausible. In any case, in the same Preface Hardy refers to Mrs Oliphant's article on the Anti-Marriage League, which as well as *Jude* discussed *The Woman Who Did*, *The British Barbarians* and *Gallia*; and in a letter to Edmund Gosse written immediately after the publication of *Jude* he plaintively attempted to deflect some of the criticism that had already been levelled at him: 'It is curious that some of the papers should look upon the novel as a manifesto on "the marriage question" (although of course it involves it) . . . I suppose the attitude of these critics is to be accounted for by the fact that, during the serial publication of my story, a sheaf of "purpose" novels on the matter appeared.'[15] (Once the critical pressure was off, he went back on this; the 1912 Preface acknowledges that the marriage question is central to the novel: 'My opinion at that time . . . was what it is now, that a marriage should be dissolved as soon as it becomes a cruelty to either of the partners . . . and it seemed a good foundation for the fable of tragedy'.) Hardy had met both Grant Allen and Ménie Muriel Dowie; he owned a copy of *The Woman Who Did*, and Sarah Grand had sent him *The Heavenly Twins* as 'a very inadequate acknowledgement of all she owes to his genius'. Even so, it might be argued that the heroines of these novels, being mostly of the pure rather than the neurotic school, are less like Sue Bridehead than the New Women of the George Egerton model. However, Hardy had not only read *Keynotes*, but had been sufficiently impressed by it to copy out lengthy passages into his notebook. Apparently he was particularly struck by George Egerton's descriptions of drunken men, her analysis of woman's 'complex nature', the latent sexuality of 'a refined, physically fragile woman', and her attacks on the 'artificial morality' which has made 'moral and legal prisons based on false conceptions of sin and shame'.[16] These notes, made while he was working on the final draft of *Jude the Obscure*, have obvious relevance to his own novel. Most of the passages come from the story 'A Cross Line', whose intelligent, sensitive and vividly imaginative heroine is married to a worthy man who bores and irritates her. She gives as her reasons for marrying so unsuitably 'it isn't the love, you know, it's the being loved'; and Sue excuses her marriage to Phillotson on the grounds that 'sometimes a woman's love of being loved gets the better of her conscience'. George Egerton's heroine, slender, pale and dark-haired, with 'a quivering nervous little face' is very like Sue with her 'nervous little face' and 'quivering, tender nature'; here unquestionably is an 'intellectualised, emancipated bundle of nerves' who not only pre-dates Sue Bridehead but was also well known to Hardy.

The German reviewer was innocently mistaken too in assuming that a woman novelist would not have allowed her heroine to break down at the end. Sue's career follows a pattern made familiar by the New Woman writers: theoretically emancipated to start with, she suddenly and almost inexplicably marries the wrong man, makes an initially successful bid for freedom and then collapses into crushing conformity. This is an exact parallel to the sequence of Hadria's life in *The Daughters of Danaus* and bears general similarity to the plots of other New Woman novels. Almost all New Woman heroines break down at the end, most go through some period of nervous prostration if not madness, and both Evadne and Hadria anticipate Sue in turning back to the Church in their defeat. Of course, as Hardy tiresomely reiterated in his own defence, Sue's story forms only a part of the novel's theme; it is constructed also, as he said, 'to tell . . . of a deadly war waged between flesh and spirit; and to point the tragedy of unfulfilled aims'[17]. But when Hardy told Gosse that 'the only remarks which can be said to bear on the *general* marriage question occur in dialogue, and comprise no more than half a dozen pages in a book of five hundred'[18] he was being, at best, disingenuous. Attacks on marriage pervade the commentary in the novel, and are, in Jude's marriage to Arabella and more importantly in Sue's return to Phillotson, implicit in the plot.

Apart from Sue's own anti-marriage pronouncements, which may conceivably add up to little more than six pages, there are several ways in which Hardy disparages the institution throughout the novel. Though he tried to persuade Gosse that commenting in his own voice was not one of them ('my own views are not expressed therein') it is difficult to see how he could explain away his description of Jude and Arabella's wedding:

> And so . . . the two swore that at every other time of their lives till death took them, they would assuredly believe, feel, and desire precisely as they had believed, felt, and desired during the few preceding weeks. What was as remarkable as the undertaking itself was the fact that nobody seemed at all surprised at what they swore. (Part I, ch. 9)

He also comments fairly directly on Sue's return to Phillotson – it is 'the self-sacrifice of the woman on the altar of what she was pleased to call her principles'. And when Jude begins to reflect on his matrimonial situation his thoughts are expressed in a style far closer to that of Hardy's narration than what we know of Jude's tone:

> There seemed to him . . . something wrong in a social ritual which made necessary a cancelling of well-formed schemes involving years of thought and labour, of foregoing a man's one opportunity of showing himself superior to the lower animals, and of contributing his units of work to the general progress of his generation, because of a momentary surprise by a new and transitory instinct which had nothing in it of the nature of vice, and could be only at the most called weakness. He was inclined to inquire what he had done, or she lost, for that matter, that he deserved to be caught in a gin which would cripple him, if not her also, for the rest of a lifetime? (Part I, ch. 9)

Though Jude is said at the beginning of the passage to hold these views 'vaguely and dimly' they develop into a pretty cogent argument. It sounds very much like Hardy himself speaking through his character.

On the other side, characters who express support for marriage do so in terms just as damaging as those who speak against. Arabella advises Sue to marry Jude because

> life with a man is more business-like after it, and money matters work better. And then, you see, if you have rows, and he turns you out of doors, you can get the law to protect you, which you can't otherwise. . . . And if he bolts away from you . . . you'll have the

sticks o' furniture, and won't be looked upon as a thief. (Part V, ch. 2)

Later she draws on her worldly experience to show Phillotson how wrong he was to set Sue free: 'I should have kept her chained on – her spirit for kicking would have been broke soon enough! There's nothing like bondage and a stone-deaf taskmaster for taming us women. Besides, you've got the laws on your side'. It's no wonder that Sue's conversations with Arabella make her feel 'how hopelessly vulgar an institution legal marriage is'; and the wedding ceremonies which Jude and Sue observe, patently designed to illustrate two extremes, in different ways support her judgement. The first, in the registry office, emphasises desiccated legality and squalor: the room contains 'law books in musty calf', papers 'tied with red tape' and 'iron safes'. The floor is 'stained' by the couples who have stood there, and the wedding taking place is obviously contrived to show marriage as a pathetic and sordid snatching at legalised respectability. The bride, 'sad and timid', is heavily pregnant and has a black eye; the groom, a soldier just out of prison, is 'sullen and reluctant'. The second, a church wedding of 'ordinary prettiness and interest', shows both the naivety of the undertaking – the bride gives her responses in a 'mechanical murmur of words whose meaning her brain seemed to gather not at all' – and the symbolic barbarity of its traditional trappings: 'The flowers in the bride's hand look sadly like the garland which decked the heifers of sacrifice in old times!' observes Sue.

Evidence against marriage is piled up relentlessly. We have the verbal and visible testimonies for the prosecution and, particularly through Phillotson's experience, we see how punitive is the rigidity of public opinion in its favour. His obviously humane arguments justifying his release of Sue lead Gillingham merely to the conclusion that 'she ought to be smacked and brought to her senses'. When Phillotson attempts to explain his actions to the inhabitants of Shaston he finds 'all the respectable . . . and well-to-do fellow-natives' against him 'to a man' and his only supporters the itinerant fairground and market people. They, like Arabella, are part of the continual undertone of pragmatic country wisdom about marriage which is based not on reasoned argument or moral conviction but the exigencies of bitter experience. Here rigid convention meets cheerfully undisciplined amorality, the rector is given a bloody nose by a chimney-sweep and rationality is left broken and impotent in the middle. Curiously, though, all sides, whatever their opinions on the sanctity of marriage, apparently accept without question that it invariably makes people miserable. Arabella, observing Jude and Sue's undisguised affection and 'complete mutual understanding', reflects 'O no – I fancy they are not married, or they wouldn't be so much to one another as that'. When Sue returns from her second unsuccessful attempt to marry Jude and openly calls herself Mrs Fawley the neighbours are convinced that her claim is legitimate by 'her dull, cowed, and listless manner'. And by the end of the novel this insistence that unhappiness is the only guarantee of a legal marriage becomes almost absurd. Jude and Arabella, once more united in Christminster, arouse the suspicion of their landlord, who

> had doubted if they were married at all, especially as he had seen Arabella kiss Jude one evening when she had taken a little cordial: and he was about to give them notice to quit, till by chance overhearing her one night haranguing Jude in rattling terms, and ultimately flinging a shoe at his head, he recognised the note of genuine wedlock; and concluding that they must be respectable, said no more. (Part VI, ch. 8)

It is true that Hardy does not consistently argue the case against marriage in his own voice. Instead he jabs repeatedly with the blunt instrument of tired cynicism – often a crude irritant where open polemic could have thrust the point home.

However, we still have Sue Bridehead, with her New Woman characteristics and the anti-marriage arguments from which Hardy tried to dissociate himself. Robert Gittings, in his generally excellent biography *Young Thomas Hardy*, argues that contemporary critics were mistaken in seeing Sue as a New Woman of the 1890s:[19] 'In reality', he says, 'she is much more what was called "The Girl of the Period" in the 1860s'. Gittings has picked an unfortunate descriptive label – the Girl of the Period, characterised by Mrs Lynn Linton as a powder-caked man-hunter, could scarcely be further removed from Sue – but the evidence he cites for seeing her as an advanced woman of an earlier period is interesting. Sue's objections to religion are, as Gittings says, cast very much in the positivist terms of Comte and do indeed belong more typically to the sixties than the nineties. But a general revolt against Christianity was as much a feature of the New Woman as of the advanced woman of the sixties, and in any case Sue's anti-religious feelings seem to be contrived more for their effect on Jude than as a central part of her character. As Jude's interest in Sue builds up during his early days in Christminster we find a sudden and clumsily prepared insistence on his piety. Before meeting Sue he continually thinks of her as a companion in his devotions. Watching her illuminating texts in the shop where she works he reflects that hers is 'a sweet, saintly, Christian business'; later he yearns for her as 'a companion in Anglican worship', 'steeped body and soul in church sentiment as she must be by occupation and habit'. As we are already enlightened as to Sue's actual convictions, we know that disillusionment on this point is being prepared as inexorably as Jude's rejection by the university. Secondly, Gittings points out that Sue is less concerned about career opportunities than many New Women of the nineties, but in stating that she is not 'striving for . . . economic independence' and that she 'accepts the very minor jobs then allotted to women' he is not taking full account of what she says about her work. After all, she agrees to go back to teaching (in which she excels) and to train properly in order to become a partner to Phillotson; and also she sees even professional teaching as a retrograde step: 'I resolved . . . to get into an occupation in which I shall be more independent', she says, and 'I was getting on as an art-designer'. But Gittings's third argument, that Sue belongs to the sixties rather than the nineties because she 'quotes Mill even obsessively' (only twice, actually) and 'by the 1890s, Mill was out of date' is clearly wrong. Mill was standard reading for the New Woman heroine – Evadne, Jessamine and Gallia are all specifically said to have been influenced by him.

Sue's resemblance to the New Woman heroines of popular fiction emerges in a variety of ways. As we have noted in the previous chapter, one of her fundamental objections to marriage – that 'it is as culpable to bind yourself to love always as to believe a creed always, and as silly as to vow always to like a particular food or drink' – is an echo of Shelley which reverberated through the New Woman novels. Also, her view of marriage as a purely civil undertaking, reflecting no divine or even human morality, is a common feature of the anti-marriage heroine. Hadria, in the course of one of her many arguments with her sister-in-law, proclaims that 'what you call the "contract" is simply a cunning contrivance for making a woman and her possible children the legal property of a man, and for enlisting her own honour and conscience to safeguard the disgraceful transaction'. And Sue feels that her honour and conscience should allow her to be released from marriage 'if it is only a sordid contract, based on material convenience in householding, rating, and taxing, and the inheritance of land and money by children, making it necessary that the male parent should be known'. Her shrinking from sex, partly, of course, a personal peculiarity, can also be turned against the conventions of marriage: 'What tortures me so much is the necessity of being responsive to this man whenever he wishes . . . the dreadful contract to feel in a particular way in a matter whose very essence is its voluntariness'. Hardy explained to Gosse what is not made clear in the novel, that one of Sue's reasons for refusing to marry Jude is that 'while uncontracted she feels at liberty to yield herself as seldom as she chooses',[20] and the same distinction in dignity between wife and mistress had been made by George Egerton: 'Man demands from a wife as a right, what he must sue from a mistress as a favour, until marriage becomes for many women a legal prostitution, a nightly degradation'. Gwen Waring too, we may remember, feels that 'this one flesh business' is 'a horrid thing'.

Many smaller details also combine to suggest links which could have been picked up by contemporary readers. Sue's list of reading, for example, which seems so striking in the context of Hardy's other novels – 'Lemprière, Catullus, Martial, Juvenal . . . De Foe, Smollett, Fielding, Shakespeare' – looks much less extraordinary when set against Evadne's literary feats and the learned researches of other New Women. The curious scene in which Sue wades through the river and sits with Jude talking intimately in the middle of the night, wet, shivering and dressed in his clothes, is very reminiscent of Angelica's escapade with the Tenor in *The Heavenly Twins*. There is nothing like a good soaking and a touch of transvestism for loosening a New Woman's tongue, we infer. Also, Sue's deliberate and somewhat callous experimenting with emotions was a characteristic of the New Woman noted by many critics. When Sue hauls Jude into the church where he is later to give her away in marriage to Phillotson she contritely explains that this heartlessness derives from her 'curiosity to hunt up a new sensation', just as Gwen Waring, willing to investigate any new emotional situation, marries because 'I like new sensations. I am curious'. Even the death of Sue's children, seized upon by countless critics as one of the most obviously crude and preposterous aspects of the novel, is in line with the bizarre treatment meted out to many a New Woman's offspring. George Egerton takes infanticide quite coolly in *Discords*; Edith Beale in *The Heavenly Twins* produces a diseased little monster, and

Jessamine Halliday is driven mad when her children kill each other. Indeed, contemporary reviewers of *Jude* seemed to take far greater exception to the stuck pig than to the hanged children.

Hardy is very much in tune with the times in lavishing so much attention on his heroine's sexuality, but there seems to be a certain amount of confusion in his treatment of what he termed Sue's 'unusually weak and fastidious' instincts. Her lack of sensuality is in part simply an aspect of her character; in addition it has a polemical force in stressing the misguidedness of Sue's return to Phillotson, when she offers herself like a sacrificial victim and is carried with clenched teeth to the bed; and partly it is used schematically to chart the flesh-spirit dichotomy in Jude. That Sue should have any sort of relationship with Phillotson is in itself scarcely credible, and Hardy wastes little effort in attempting to make it so. When Jude sees Phillotson walking home with his arm round Sue's waist it is as much a surprise to the reader as to Jude, and is felt by both to be just another knife-twisting irony: 'The ironical clinch to his sorrow was given by the thought that the intimacy between his cousin and the schoolmaster had been brought about entirely by himself'. Hardy shoves Sue into a totally unsuitable engagement mainly in order to make Jude writhe; it is only after the marriage, with Sue's skulkings in cubby-holes and dramatic leap from the window, that we begin to appreciate the relationship from her point of view. The other thematic function of her sexual coldness – the contrast with Arabella's animal sensuality – is also contrived largely for its effect on Jude. He at least sees his platonic relationship with Sue as proof of his ability to overcome a propensity to vice:

> All that's best and noblest in me loves you, and your freedom from everything that's gross has elevated me, and enabled me to do what I should never have dreamt myself capable of, or any man, a year or two ago. It is all very well to preach about self-control, and the wickedness of coercing a woman. But I should just like a few of the virtuous people who have condemned me in the past, about Arabella and other things, to have been in my tantalizing position with you these late weeks! – they'd believe, I think, that I have exercised some little restraint in always giving in to your wishes – living here in one house, and not a soul between us. (Part V, ch. 2)

He almost seems to be praising himself for not having raped her.

But this idea that Sue's freedom from everything that is gross has an ennobling effect goes very much against other things in the novel. When Arabella's grossness tempts Jude it is, as he says, to something which 'had nothing in it of the nature of vice, and could be only at the most called weakness'. More importantly, Sue herself would theoretically condemn this point of view: in her convictions she seems to be a New Woman of the free-love persuasion. She responds to Jude's tender assurance that he believes her claim to have retained her virginity in her relationship with the undergraduate with a characteristic sneer at both Jude and herself — 'better women would not'. When Jude comes round to a position where he would much prefer to be praising her for the opposite behaviour she again insists on withholding herself sexually while arguing for the free-love ideal:

> I *may* feel as well as you that I have a perfect right to live with you as you thought – from this moment. I *may* hold the opinion that, in a proper state of society, the father of a woman's child will be as much a private matter of hers as the cut of her under-linen, on whom nobody will have the right to question her. (Part IV, ch. 5)

An unfortunate analogy, perhaps, – in such circumstances the cut of her underclothes would scarcely be a byword for privacy – but the theory is very advanced indeed. Still, as Jude points out, Sue's theory is usually far ahead of her practice, and these things would be consistent with her character were it not for the way in which, after the death of the children, she reflects on her past relationship with Jude. Apparently at some stage theory and practice had ideally coalesced:

> We went about loving each other too much – indulging ourselves to utter selfishness with each other! We said – do you remember? – that we would make a virtue of joy. I said it was Nature's intention, Nature's law and *raison d'être* that we should be joyful in what instincts she afforded us – instincts which civilisation had taken upon itself to thwart. (Part VI, ch. 2)

This is not the Sue Bridehead who combines sexual provocation with frigidity, but an apparently honest and fulfilled New Woman who has succeeded in practising what she preached. Unfortunately Sue is remembering herself as a character whom the reader has never been granted the privilege of seeing; presumably all this occurs during the period, quickly glossed over in the novel, when Sue is bearing her children and when, as Hardy helpfully informs us, 'the twain were happy – between their times of sadness'. By the end of the novel, in her desertion of Jude and return to Phillotson, Sue is being condemned for deviating from a position we have never really witnessed her holding.

This seems to point to one of the novel's major weaknesses: its main themes and ideas are sketched out with reasonable clarity, but are not filled in with sufficient supportive evidence, or else become blurred by conflicting reports on the characters, particularly Sue. When she creeps off through the symbolic fog to rejoin Phillotson, Hardy comments 'the blow of her bereavement seemed to have destroyed her reasoning faculty. The once keen vision was dimmed', and hyperbolic testimonies to the power of her intellect are given by both Phillotson and Jude. Poor Phillotson confesses himself thoroughly routed in debate – 'I can't answer her arguments – she has read ten times as much as I. Her intellect sparkles like diamonds, while mine smoulders like brown paper. . . . She's one too many for me!' – and Jude apostrophises her as 'a woman-poet, a woman-seer, a woman whose soul shone like a diamond – whom all the wise of the world would have been proud of, if they could have known you'. But while it is true that Sue is in the habit of lobbing unreturnable quotations across the breakfast table, and of delivering searing criticisms of Christminster and the Church (most of which, as she admits, have been picked up from her undergraduate friend), her behaviour is determined almost entirely by emotional caprice. On the one hand, Hardy seems to be building her up into a model of the New Womanhood in her theory, and on the other, he shows her as, in his terms, an entirely typical feminine woman in her practice. And Sue, as the unfortunate embodiment of these two extremes, is shrewd enough to analyse her behaviour but apparently powerless to alter it. Explaining to Jude why she married Phillotson, she says:

Sometimes a woman's *love of being loved* gets the better of her conscience, and though she is agonised at the thought of treating a man cruelly, she encourages him to love her while she doesn't love him at all. Then, when she sees him suffering, her remorse sets in, and she does what she can to repair the wrong. (Part IV, ch. 5)

And when Jude, with some justification, glosses this as 'you simply mean that you flirted outrageously with him, poor old chap, and then repented' she characteristically dissolves into the tears which she knows will avert further criticism. It is interesting too that though at first it is Arabella who performs the function of distracting the hero from his higher purposes, later on Sue actually confesses to acting the part of the typical Hardy heroine: 'O I seem so bad – upsetting men's courses like this!'. In Sue more than in any of the other heroines we feel Hardy's conception of women pulling against his desire to expound theories about social organisation. But that Hardy was very much more in favour of Sue's ideas than he cared to admit at the time may be judged from a letter he wrote to Mrs Fawcett some ten years later:

> I have for a long time been in favour of woman-suffrage. . . . I am in favour of it because I think the tendency of the woman's vote will be to break up the pernicious conventions in respect of women, customs, religion, illegitimacy, the stereotyped house-hold (that it must be the unit of society), the father of a woman's child (that it is anybody's business but the woman's own) . . . slaughter-houses (that they should be dark dens of cruelty), and other matters which I got into hot water for touching on many years ago.[21]

While it is doubtful whether Arabella's vote would have gone against slaughter-houses – and, of course, demonstrably untrue that the mass of women ever voted for the social reforms Hardy outlines – this does suggest that he was to some degree seeing Sue as a portent for a better future. As she says herself when watching with shuddering distaste the pretty church wedding, 'everybody is getting to feel as we do. We are a little beforehand, that's all'.

Hardy was displaying touching restraint in saying merely that he 'got into hot water' for writing on such topics. *Jude the Obscure* provoked almost hysterically abusive reactions from much of the press. The *Pall Mall Gazette* reviewed it under the heading 'Jude the Obscene' and summed it up as 'dirt, drivel and damnation'.[22] Mrs Oliphant opined that 'there may be books more disgusting, more impious as regards human nature, more foul in detail, in those dark corners where the amateurs of filth find garbage to their taste; but not . . . from any Master's hand'.[23] The *Athenaeum* judged some of the characters 'nothing less than loathsome and repulsive in the highest degree'[24] and the *Guardian* claimed that the whole novel 'affects one like a shameful nightmare'.[25]

There were, though, several glowing reviews, notably from Edmund Gosse in *Cosmopolis*, Havelock Ellis in the *Savoy*, and from the *Saturday Review* and *Westminster Review*. Apart from the obvious difference in evaluation between those for and against the novel, the most significant distinction appears in the way the two camps see *Jude the Obscure* relating to other novels. Those who praised it consistently dissociated it from contemporary movements; those who attacked it saw it as part of the New Woman fiction. Mrs Oliphant provides the clearest example of the second category, but as we have seen, Robert Tyrrell also flatly dismissed *Jude* as just another New Woman novel – 'It differs in no wise from the "hill-top" novels, save in the note of distinction and the power of touch which must discriminate Mr Hardy at his worst from the Grant Allens and Iotas at their best'.[26] The *World* called Arabella – quite inaccurately – the 'Wessex Woman Who Did', and, obviously pleased with this witticism, went on to mock Sue as 'the Woman Who Can't' and 'the Woman Who Won't', concluding that Hardy had 'consciously or unconsciously thrown the whole weight of his powerful literary influence into the scale of revolting womanhood à la Lanchester'.[27] (Miss Lanchester was a woman who really did, running away from her parents amidst a blaze of publicity to live in unmarried bliss with her lover. The story was blown up by the press as an example of the pernicious influence of New Woman novels.) A. J. Butler in the *National Review* saw Hardy being 'caught in the fashion of the period' and in a veiled reference to Keynotes novels warned that 'there is nothing more certain in literature than that a tendency to dwell on foul details has never been a "note" of any but third-rate work'.[28] And the *Critic* saw Sue as a 'type now becoming familiar in fiction' and the whole novel as 'an especially good specimen of a class of literature which has of late years come as a disturbing element into English fiction'.[29]

On the other side, D. F. Hannigan in the *Westminster Review* specifically dissociated Sue – and indeed all Hardy's heroines – from 'the objectionable crowd of so-called "advanced" women';[30] Richard le Gallienne in the *Idler* denied the anti-marriage league accusations: 'Too many reviewers have treated *Jude* as a polemic against marriage. Nothing could be more unjust';[31] and Edmund Gosse commiserated with Hardy on the accident of his novel appearing just after 'a sheaf of "purpose" stories on the "marriage question"' and ventured the opinion, promptly proved wrong, that 'no serious critic . . . will accuse Mr Hardy of joining the ranks of these deciduous troublers of our peace'.[32] Finally, the *Saturday Review* offered some interesting observations on the decline of the New Woman fiction and the swing in public taste:

> It is now the better part of a year ago since the collapse of the 'New Woman' fiction began. The success of *The Woman Who Did* was perhaps the last of a series of successes attained . . . by works dealing intimately and unrestrainedly with sexual affairs. It marked a crisis. A respectable public had for a year or more read such books eagerly, and discussed hitherto unheard of topics with burning ears and an air of liberality. The reviewers had reviewed in the spirit of public servants. But . . . the pendulum bob of public conscience swung back swiftly and forcibly. . . . And the reviewers . . . have changed with the greatest dexterity from a chorus praising 'outspoken purity' to a band of public informers against indecorum. . . . A period of terror, analogous to that of the New England Witch Mania, is upon us.[33]

Though there seems to be some exaggeration here of the tolerance afforded the New Woman novels, it is certainly true that some sort of reaction had set in. The *Spectator* in its article '"Hill-Top Novels" and the Morality of Art' was much harder on *The Heavenly Twins* than when reviewing it three years earlier. And Mrs Oliphant, who in her review of *Tess* had stated that up to the time of the heroine's return to D'Urberville 'poor little Tess . . . has nothing but our pity' and 'we do not object to the defiant blazon of a Pure Woman',[34] changed her tune considerably in 'The Anti-Marriage League': 'To demonstrate that a woman, twice fallen from the woman's code of honour and purity, was by that fact proved to be specially and aggressively pure, was a task for a Hercules, and Mr Hardy has no more succeeded in doing this than others have done before him'. Certainly *Jude the Obscure* marked the virtual end of the New Woman fiction as it existed in the nineties.

By following a relatively clear development in his own work Hardy had arrived at a position where he appeared to be crowning a popular movement with his august literary name. The question of direct influence from minor writers cannot be definitely solved, but it seems safe to say at least that his earlier interest in matters of sexual behaviour and the nature of marriage should have made him particularly susceptible to the feminist ideas that were in the air when he wrote *Jude*. It is interesting to note too that the German reviewer's definition of Sue as a 'woman of the feminist movement' is neither denied nor qualified by Hardy. Indeed we may wonder how many of these comments can legitimately be attributed to the anonymous reviewer; some of the phrases used in the lengthy description of Sue – 'licensed to be loved on the premises', for example – are actually Hardy's own and appear in the novel itself. Clearly Hardy is thinking of Sue as a distinctively modern product, and there is ample evidence to justify the assumption of so many contemporary readers that she is another New Woman heroine: perhaps it was only the more perceptive, or more sympathetic, who saw also the features which mark her affinity with Hardy's earlier and less alarming women. But Hardy was not the only novelist of repute to be caught up in the New Woman question. As the *Athenaeum* sourly observed in its review of *Jude*, 'Mr Meredith has triumphantly shown' that even the 'dreary question of the marriage tie and its permanence'[35] can deserve a place in fiction, and it is to the works of Meredith and Gissing that we shall turn in the next chapter.

4 Meredith and Gissing: Fair Ladies in Revolt and Odd Women

Meredith and Gissing may seem an unlikely combination. Meredith's novels, presided over by the self-consciously sparkling and sometimes rather fey Comic Spirit and written in a style described by the *Spectator* as 'affectedly grotesque', contrast starkly with Gissing's avowed 'savagery' and his grim and dogged pursuit of the real. Meredith, lionised towards the end of his life as the grand old man of English letters, the greatest of living novelists, has since slid steadily into a decent obscurity; Gissing, treated with wary respect by his contemporaries but never popular in his lifetime, now commands a growing band of devoted admirers and has been the subject of several recent studies. Yet both have consistently been regarded – when regarded at all – as champions of women. Richard le Gallienne, in the first full-length book on Meredith, declared that 'there can be no doubt that woman has yet had no such ally in her battle against masculinity as he'.[1] The *Bookman* found that Meredith 'has . . . his warmest admirers among women. Some of them hold him to be their best interpreter'.[2] And Laurence Housman rallied all suffragettes to the Meredith flag: ' "Meredith", wrote Stevenson, "is my leader, and I fight under his colours." And those who are working for Women's Suffrage might well make that phrase their own'.[3] Gissing's 'desire for the emancipation of women from their ignorance and subserviency' was noted by Frank Swinnerton in 1924;[4] the *Spectator* remarked on his similarity to the New Woman novelists – 'The "Heavenly Twins" themselves could hardly desire doctrines more advanced'[5] – and at least one critic was reduced to breathless eulogy in the face of his brilliant depiction of women: 'We are amazed at the remarkable collection of women whom he presents. The men are interesting . . . but the women are remarkable! Who but Meredith has drawn a galaxy of portraits equally as fine!'[6] Meredith professed warm admiration for Gissing's work; and in the false marriage in *Denzil Quarrier* Gissing clearly betrays the influence of Meredith's *One of Our Conquerors*. In their treatment of the woman question these two widely differing novelists have much in common.

Like Hardy, both Meredith and Gissing had personal reasons for taking up the anti-marriage cudgels. Meredith's acutely unhappy experiences during the breakdown of his marriage to Mary, daughter of Thomas Love Peacock, are recorded in his poem *Modern Love*; his second marriage, to a woman by all accounts far less interesting and intelligent than Mary Peacock, was, however, tranquil and apparently happy. Gissing displayed an almost suicidal impulse to choose the wrong mate. Nell Harrison, for whom he stole money from the cloakrooms at Owens College, brought him a month's hard labour, a permanent stop to what promised to be a brilliant academic career, and a thoroughly miserable marriage. Edith Underwood, whom Gissing picked up in the street after Nell's death, proved herself a hopelessly incompetent mother and house-keeper, and, when her screaming temper tipped her over into what could reasonably be diagnosed as madness, was confined to an asylum. Finally Gissing did what so many advanced thinkers of the nineties advocated, and lived in free union with the Frenchwoman Gabrielle Fleury, until his death. Reports on this last love differ widely – Wells, for one, was open in his dislike of her – but Gissing was clearly determined to adore her if he starved in the attempt.[7] Both writers produced what in the climate of the nineties could be regarded as anti-marriage novels (*Lord Ormont and his Aminta, The Odd Women* and *The Whirlpool*) and neither was as reticent as Hardy in expressing views on women and marriage outside fiction. Both Meredith and Gissing were fervent advocates of education as the key to female emancipation. 'More brain, O Lord, more brain!' moaned Meredith in *Modern Love* (and then went on to marry a woman of sweetly docile but almost totally unintellectual charac-ter). And the letters which Gissing wrote to his two unmarried sisters frequently contained the most ruthlessly erudite reading-lists which, it seems fairly clear, they had neither the ability nor the inclination to follow.

Meredith's opinions on female emancipation were reasonably consistent. Whether talking about marriage or work he always came back to the necessity of education. 'I have this feeling for women, because, what with nature and the world, they are the most heavily burdened', he wrote to Miss Price. 'I can foresee great and blessed changes for the race when they have achieved independence; for that must come of the exercise of their minds.'[8] And again, when asked by the *Daily Mail* for a contribution to its series 'The Marriage Handicap', he wrote: 'The fault at the bottom of the business is that women are so uneducated, so unready'.[9] (His solution to the marriage problem consisted of a compromise between free love and conventional wedlock – marriage should be based on contracts renewable every ten years or so, an idea which crops up also in *One of Our Conquerors*.) But Meredith was always adamant that no move for female equality should be at the expense of woman's 'natural' refinement and delicacy, and he lived long enough to see his ideal of the free-spirited, courageous but still essentially feminine woman threatened, in his view, by the wilder antics of the suffragettes. An innocently amusing article by a *Daily Telegraph* reporter, who had managed to inveigle himself into the Meredith household on the day of the great man's eightieth birthday, records the ageing novelist's views on these rampantly modern women. Written fairly clearly between the lines of this article is the fact that Meredith, frail, deaf and crotchety, was, when persuaded to utter at all, disconcertingly rambling in his replies, but a question on suffrage goaded him suddenly into coherence:

> Suffragists! . . . I have always stood up for the intellectual capacities of woman. I like to see the combative spirit in them. It is as it should be. Certainly they should be given the use of intellectual weapons. But I am not in agreement with anything that is bad taste and bad strategy. Those rowdy scenes! No! Not that. That is not the way. There is a better. [10]

Though it is never made clear what this better way is (apparently exhausted by so much relevant speech, he slides off into a mumbling disquisition on the Napoleonic Wars) the sentiment typifies Meredith's attitude towards women: good taste at all costs, the battle to be waged and won in the intellectual arena.

Meredith's novels, for good reasons, are not much read nowadays. Though he is clearly a writer of great penetration and psychological sensitivity, it is rare that the illuminations he offers are not obscured by the sometimes impenetrable mannerisms of his style. Occasionally, as in *The Egoist*, style and subject can combine into a brilliant formal subtlety, but more often his wilful complexity of expression and his oblique narrative method lead merely to confused obfuscation. Meredith himself confessed that 'women who read my books have much to surmount in the style',[11] but why he should imagine that this difficulty is confined to his female readers is hard to understand. Certainly those reviewers – predominantly male – who were not a party to the astonishing inflation of his reputation during the eighties and nineties repeatedly admitted to being utterly baffled by the Meredithian manner. The *Spectator*, affecting pained surprise as each new novel was acclaimed by its competitors, finally broke down and simply pronounced *The Amazing Marriage* 'terribly hard reading for the natural man'.[12] The *Athenaeum's* reviewer was stunned by the style: 'After one has been stung with a whip, or battered on the brain with a quarterstaff, it is not the pretty wrist play nor the artful bludgeoning that gets the praise; before praise is mentioned, there is something to say of the smarting weals, of the aching bumps on the skull'.[13] And the *Saturday Review* offered a very creditable parody:

> The taste for Mr George Meredith's later novels is a sentiment personal, freakish, tiptoeing an impertinent superiority of glance. From a pinnacle of the supercilious it twinkles a cavalier stare: – below, the swinish; above – the stars![14]

One sees the problem.

Still, Meredith's novels were widely read and, it seems, greatly appreciated by contemporary women of advanced views. Edith Slater, who dismissed Hardy's heroines as 'men's women', had nothing but praise for Meredith – 'he, better than any man, feels for the sufferings and limitations of the sex'[15] – and it is not difficult to see why. Though his fictional treatment of women follows a pattern very similar to Hardy's, with his early, sometimes tentatively expressed, convictions suddenly bursting out into explicitly formulated problems in the nineties, there is never anything like the same tension in his work between an essentially conventional view of women and a radical stance on social and sexual questions. Meredith always portrayed women who could cope with freedom, and when in the nineties it was offered in fiction if not in fact, he showed them seizing it eagerly. Though his own novels are bewildering in their artificiality of expression, his most consistent plea for women was that they should be 'natural'. Once women have shaken off the false trappings draped round them they will at once become more natural and more like men, an idea expressed with rare succinctness in his poem 'A Ballad of Fair Ladies in Revolt':

> But O how different from reality
> Men's fiction is! how like you in the plan,
> Is woman, knew you her as we!

And Cecilia Halkett in *Beauchamp's Career* (1875) epitomises all that Meredith most disliked in conventional woman. She is

> one of the artificial creatures called women . . . who dare not be spontaneous, and cannot act independently if they would continue to be admirable in the world's eye, and who for that object must remain fixed on shelves, like other marketable wares, avoiding motion to avoid shattering or tarnishing. This is their fate, only in degree less inhuman than that of Hellenic and Trojan princesses offered up to the Gods, or pretty slaves to the dealers. Their artificiality is at once their bane and their source of superior pride. (ch. 32)

Meredith's early novels contain a glittering array of brave, intelligent women, unfettered by the traditional bonds of artifice. Emilia – also known, confusingly, as Sandra Belloni and Vittoria – represents the quintessence of the natural woman: 'She is half man . . . she is not what man has made of your sex; and she is brave of heart'. Similarly Princess Ottilia, in *Harry Richmond* (1871), 'moved free as air. She could pursue her studies, and argue and discuss and quote, keep unclouded eyes, and laugh and play, and be her whole living self'. And in the same novel, Janet Ilchester appears as the Meredithian ideal mate, a woman who, while remaining distinctively feminine, can be a companion to a man in all his activities: 'A woman who can be a friend of men is the right sort of woman to make a match with. . . . Janet Ilchester's the only girl alive who'll double the man she marries'.

After *Beauchamp's Career*, two changes in Meredith's novels can be noted which have great significance for his treatment of women. The first is a shift towards making a woman the focus of the story. The earlier novels had tended to place the hero rather comfortably at the centre of a whirling galaxy of beauties with conflicting claims to his attention, and allowed him, generally, to reach out at the end and pluck the best. From *The Egoist* onwards it is the women who occupy the central position, and increasingly the plot is constructed to illustrate some aspect of the woman question. The second is the factor of class or social respectability. While the earlier novels dangle the women as brilliant matches before the more or less deserving heroes, the later ones make the heroine slightly lower down the social scale than the man initially selected as her partner, or if not strictly lower socially, then with some kink in the family's line of respectability. Thus when these women break away from their first partner they are forced also to discard some of the conventional notions of a 'good match', and, in varying degrees, to investigate the social code which has pumped such ideas into them.

Of these novels, *Diana of the Crossways* (1885) is the most overtly feminist in subject matter, being based rather loosely on the life of Caroline Norton. But it is a work which fails in the promised largeness. Diana may dream of 'accepting martyrdom, becoming the first martyr of the modern woman's cause – a grand position!' but in fact her deprivations amount to little more than riding in a third-class railway compartment and living alone in lodgings. By these means she hopes 'to prove . . . that a woman can walk . . . independent of the common reserves and artifices'. And although Meredith expends a great deal of energy in trying to build her into a model of wit and intellect she amounts in the end to little more than an unusually attractive combination of feminine weakness and masculine mind. She is just the kind of exceptional woman who would appeal to the intelligent Victorian reader – glittering and untouchable, yet at the same time endearingly fallible, pronouncing epigrams over dinner and churning out competent light fiction, yet clearly in need of a man's firm guidance when it comes to the real economic or political stuff of life. In the end she settles suddenly into a cosy marriage, a conclusion which Meredith himself confessed to being unsatisfactory: 'Diana of the Crossways keeps me still on her sad last way to wedlock. I could have killed her merrily, with my compliments to the public; and that was my intention. But the marrying of her, sets me traversing feminine labyrinths, and . . . the why of it can never be accounted for'.[16]

The three novels which Meredith produced in the nineties all follow the fashion in exploring some aspect of the marriage question. *The Amazing Marriage* (1895) is so bizarre as to numb the reader into bored incredulity. Its basic situation, improbable enough in itself, is to marry off an athletic and stolidly humourless young girl to the most eligible man in England, Lord Fleetwood. He then promptly repents of his folly and deserts her, returning only once, via a ladder and her bedroom window, to conceive their child. Her subsequent career takes her to a Welsh mining village, where she dispenses charity and cheer, and to the Spanish War, where she fights shoulder to shoulder with her brother, thus achieving the independence demanded of amazingly married heroines in the nineties. *One of Our Conquerors* (1891) is a novel of deliberate and infuriating obscurity, but one which nevertheless, particularly in its heroines, contains some fine characterisation. It deals with two themes which were later given more stark treatment by the New Woman novelists: the first, what Meredith himself termed 'the great Marriage Question', and the second the problem of 'purity'. Victor Radnor, because of his foolish marriage in youth to a woman much older than himself, is forced to live in free union with what society takes to be his wife, Nataly. Their problem is to raise the daughter of their irregular liaison, Nesta, in ignorance of her parents' misconduct and to marry her off respectably before anybody gets wind of the fact that, though herself innocent, she could not conventionally be termed pure. In Nataly, Meredith has captured the nice paradox of a woman whose circumstances compel her to be in conflict with the social code, but whose personality inclines her towards implicit conformity. Herself a victim of Victor's rash and hasty marriage, she nevertheless sees salvation for her daughter lying only in a quick snatch at a suitable mate. If this is to be successful, Nesta must be kept 'pure', ignorant in particular of her parents' marital situation and in general of all sexual matters. Nataly becomes, as Meredith points out, typical of an English motherhood which is compelled 'to worship in the concrete an hypocrisy it abhors in the abstract'. Victor too wants Nesta to be married, 'to have her protected, secure with the world warm about her', but has less confidence in the equation of ignorance with purity:

Repression and mystery, he considered wholesome for girls; and he considered the enlightening of them – to some extent – a prudential measure for their defence . . . also the facts of current human life in the crude of the reports or the crooked of the sermon in the newspapers, are a noxious diet for our daughters; whom nevertheless we cannot hope to be feeding always on milk: and there is a time when their adorable pretty ignorance . . . is harmful: – but how beautiful the shining simplicity of our dear young English girls! (ch. 14)

The result of this muddle is that Victor sends Nesta away to have her purity reinforced by his maiden aunts and some bracing sea air. The outcome is fitting: Nesta is dosed with purity by the aunts, and regaled with stories of the real world by a fallen woman, and she begins to conceive 'revolutionary ideas of the duties of women, and their powers'. But in the end it takes a man, the energetically radical Dartrey Fenellan, to cut through all this confusion. He sweeps down on Nataly with a contemptuous lecture against her notions of respectability and carries off Nesta to a married life of excitement and dynamic radicalism. We are left with the final irony of Nataly disapproving of the daughter who is pledged to fight the very prejudices which have blighted her mother's life. In theory, the novel attacks the social conventions of marriage and purity; but it is interesting to note that the practice which would overtly challenge them is left to the future. Dartrey and Nesta will fight, but from the secure platform of their own marital respectability.

But the novel which most clearly shows Meredith adopting the New Woman rhetoric of the nineties is *Lord Ormont and his Aminta* (1894). Here we find much anti-marriage fervour, and a solution which sends off hero and heroine to work together and live in free love. And although *Lord Ormont* is not one of Meredith's better efforts artistically, it has much in common in theme with what is probably his best novel, *The Egoist*. In these two novels, as with Hardy, we see earlier interests being up-dated and polemically strengthened in the freedom of the nineties. Both novels contrast their two main male figures according to traditional ideals of the masculine. Sir Willoughby Patterne, the egoist, is a grotesque amalgam of male prejudices who finally loses his betrothed to the far less obviously eligible Vernon Whitford, the poor relation in the great house, a tutor and scholar. In *Lord Ormont*, the crusty old peer of the title, erstwhile hero of British youth for his military exploits and uncompromising ruggedness, is forced to relinquish his Aminta to the gentle and impoverished young man whom he has employed to tidy up the spelling and grammar of his memoirs. Clara exchanges her passport into the gentry and settled opulent comfort for a roaming life and intellectual companionship, and Aminta cashes in her social ticket as Countess of Ormont for the title of fallen woman and schoolmistress. Both women are brought to see the charms of men whom their first choices would undoubtedly have pronounced cissy, and both learn to appreciate the value of equality with their men. The difference is that *The Egoist* stays just within the bounds of received morality, while *Lord Ormont and his Aminta* determinedly tramples them down.

The Egoist (1879) could have been the greatest of all anti-marriage novels. It is a masterpiece of the subtle interaction of characters within a strict social code shown to be absurdly constricting to the freedom of women, and it is only, one feels, the conventions of the time which dictate that the code should be represented by formal betrothal rather than marriage. Everything in the novel is constructed to make the engagement of Clara to Sir Willoughby appear as close an equivalent to actual marriage as possible. Clara, blinded by Willoughby's ardent wooing and masculine grace, plights her troth to him as solemnly as if she were in church: 'I am yours forever, I swear it. I will never swerve from it, I am your wife in heart, yours utterly'. And Sir Willoughby is not the only character in the novel to take this as final. Mrs Mountstuart tells Clara 'why, you are at the Church-door with him! . . . The Church-door is as binding as the altar to an honourable girl', an opinion confirmed by Dr Middleton, Clara's father: 'Why, she is as good as married. She is at the altar. . . . She is out of the market'. During her engagement Clara is actually living in Willoughby's house; the two share the guardianship of a child, the young Crossjay; and significantly Meredith devotes more care to the analysis of the physical relationship than in any other novel. Indeed the sense of their physical incompatibility is one of the main factors which fixes Clara's determination to break away. Willoughby's approaches are described in the most chilling terms:

> He enfolded her. Clara was growing hardened to it. To this she was fated; and not seeing any way to escape, she invoked a friendly frost to strike her blood, and passed through the minute unfeelingly. Having passed it, she reproached herself for making so much of it, thinking it a lesser endurance than to listen to him. (ch. 10)

A young woman who has to choose between the agony of being embraced, or the even greater torment of being talked to, by her fiancé clearly stands little chance of happiness in marriage, and Clara's horror at the situation is as compelling as anything in the

New Woman fiction: 'In a dream somehow she had committed herself to a life-long imprisonment; and, oh terror! not in a quiet dungeon; the barren walls closed round her, talked, called for ardour, expected admiration'.

Meredith plots the twists and turns of her escape attempts with immense skill. It turns into a duel between the power of masculine obduracy – Willoughby's pride reels at the thought of being jilted – and that of feminine subtlety. Honesty is useless; Clara's plain speaking is met merely with the response that Willoughby, being a man, knows her mind better than she does, and her only hope is to attempt to trick him into rejecting her. She tries, for example, to shock him into repugnancy by suggesting that she is not quite the pure young maiden he imagines. 'There is no possibility of releasing a wife', says Willoughby; 'not if she ran . . . ?' replies Clara, and Willoughby is thrown back into the comical pose of exaggerated masculine outrage at this mildest hint of impurity in his beloved:

> That she, a young lady, maiden, of strictest education, should, and without his teaching, know that wives ran! – know that by running they compelled their husbands to abandon pursuit, surrender possession! – and that she should suggest it of herself as a wife! – that she should speak of running!
>
> His ideal, the common male Egoist ideal of a waxwork sex, would have been shocked to fragments had she spoken further to fill in the outlines of these awful interjections. (ch. 15)

Clara is neatly, and, it seems, completely trapped. Her father, unable to contemplate the loss of Willoughby's vintage port which his daughter's defection would necessarily entail, refuses to listen to her pleas for sympathy, and the scene in which Clara's passionate demands for clemency are stonily refused by both together shows the ugly brutality of two men condemning a woman to misery in order to guard their own petty advantages. Clara, says Meredith, 'was not sufficiently instructed in the position of her sex to know that she had plunged herself in the thick of one of their greatest battles', but despite the more ludicrously idiosyncratic posturings of Sir Willoughby, the novel does succeed in demonstrating the typicality of the situation. The woman's final victory, however, is perhaps appropriately unheroic. Under the circumstances Clara can do little more than stick courageously to her resolve, but until Sir Willoughby decides that her punishment is to be married off ignominiously to Vernon Whitford there is a limit to how far this can carry her. Happily, what Willoughby – and the world – see as punishment, she accepts as her greatest reward, and Vernon, who has watched her growing independence with a rather stern approval, is also delighted. As in *One of Our Conquerors*, the final unconventional marriage makes up for all the previous damage done by imposed proprieties; but *The Egoist*, more tightly structured and more profitably subtle is, though out of line with its time, more perceptive about the plight of women.

Lord Ormont and his Aminta repeats the conflict between the traditional man and the buddingly rebellious woman, but this time the battle begins after, not before, marriage. The novel opens with two crocodiles of children from adjoining boys' and girls' schools watching their leaders, Aminta Farrell and Matey Weyburn, exchanging the speaking looks of calf love. Both schools, and Matey and Aminta particularly, worship the warrior-hero Lord Ormont. From the beginning attention is drawn to the schematising of masculine and feminine roles: though boys and girls are united in their admiration for military glory, the girls must yearn from afar whereas the boys can emulate. Thus when the girls come across the boys indulging in a boisterous snowball fight Meredith comments: 'The thought of the difference between themselves and the boys must have been something like a tight band – call it corset – over the chest, trying to lift and stretch for draughts of air'. Weyburn is destined to follow his father in a military career, whereas Aminta is heading for a life of stultifying decorum under the care of her aunt, but when the two meet again as adults the roles are apparently reversed; Weyburn has altered his ambitions to those of re-volutionary schoolmaster, meanwhile eking out a living as tutor and secretary, while Aminta has made a brilliant match with Lord Ormont.

However, Lord Ormont does not fulfil the expectations of schoolgirl adulation. Like Sir Willoughby, he demands complete seclusion from the world and expects his wife to enjoy it, and he too has all the repressively traditional notions of a woman's place.Though Aminta at first views with dismay what she sees as Weyburn's base ambitions, inevitably her old love begins to re-awaken and we are plunged into one of the typical marital breakdowns of the New Woman fiction. All the popular rhetoric is trundled out:

That Institution of Marriage was eyed. Is it not a halting step to happiness? It is the step of a cripple. . . . And is happiness our cry? Our cry is rather for circumstance and occasion to use our functions, and the conditions are denied to women by Marriage. (ch. 15)

Aminta 'shook her bonds in revolt from marriage', her 'pride of being chafed at the yoke of marriage', she 'regarded the wedding by law as the end a woman has to aim at, and is annihilated by hitting', 'her title was Lady Ormont: her condition actually slave'. She begins to be impressed by Weyburn's ideal of the new education, particularly in so far as it reflects on her own mistakes:

All the . . . devilry between the sexes begins at their separation. They're foreigners when they meet; and their alliances are not always binding. The chief object in life, if happiness be the aim, and the growing better than we are, is to teach men and women how to be one; for, if they're not, then each is a morsel for the other to prey on. (ch. 24)

Finally Aminta runs away from her husband, and the next step is to work in the extra-marital sexual *frisson*. Weyburn, travelling by boat to meet her, sees Aminta in the distance swimming athletically and alluringly in the sea. 'Fiery envy and desire to be alongside her set his fingers fretting at buttons' and he plunges in after her. They exchange some ecstatic commonplaces on free love, then dive under the water together, accompanied by Meredith's suggestive comment that 'there is no history of events below the surface'. After this it is all plain sailing: they go off to Switzerland to found a co-educational multinational school, and Aminta gets both mate and career. What is most remarkable about this novel, though, is that Meredith appears to have taken over the New Woman's language of propaganda without troubling to fix it very closely to his plot. Aminta declares, without hint of contradiction, that her condition is actually slave, but in most respects her marriage to Lord Ormont is quite remarkably free. In fact, since she is determined to live in England and he prefers the continent, she hardly sees him for long periods of time. Also, other elements of the story demand that the majority of its characters believe her to be unmarried anyway, and are not surprised if she acts accordingly. *Lord Ormont and his Aminta* is in every way inferior to *The Egoist*: though stuffed with the New

Woman's rhetoric it is hopelessly unsatisfactory as an embodiment of her ideals. Meredith appears to be writing fashionably but carelessly, carried along by the prevailing mode, but not really understanding it.

It would be surprising to find Gissing opening himself to the charge of being merely fashionable in his treatment of the woman question, since modishness of any kind was one of the many things he despised. In fact almost all his novels, from *Workers in the Dawn* (1880) onward, have some comments to offer on the position of women and sexual morality. *The Unclassed*, for example, written in 1884, before such topics became popular, makes its prostitute-heroine claim to be a 'pure woman' and its hero advocate – though not practise – free love. Moreover, Gissing never allowed himself to compromise with either his publishers' or his readers' demands for reticence on sexual matters. In a letter to the *Pall Mall Gazette* in 1884 he launched a vigorous attack on the 'tradesman's attitude' of contemporary writers: 'English novels are miserable stuff for a very miserable reason, simply because English novelists fear to do their best lest they should damage their popularity, and consequently their income'.[17] And he had reason to feel bitter. A novel of his own, *Mrs Grundy's Enemies*, addressed, as he said, 'to those to whom Art is dear for its own sake',[18] had proved too hot for even the notably advanced publisher Bentley to handle and never appeared in print. Of course, never having been popular and thus having little income to damage, Gissing did not stand to lose all that greatly by his artistic integrity. Unlike Hardy and Meredith, who moved steadily forward some little way in advance of public tolerance, Gissing adopted an attacking stance from the beginning and, with some minor pauses for relaxation like *The Town Traveller* or *The Paying Guest*, maintained it steadfastly throughout his career. His woman-question novels of the nineties – *The Odd Women, In the Year of Jubilee, The Whirlpool* – do not stand apart from his other work in being more outspoken or daring, but merely in making contemporary ideas about feminism and marriage the focus of the plot.

Gissing, as everyone – including himself – would agree, is a novelist of strong views. One of the most remarkable features of his work is how difficult it is to establish what these views are. True, he is supremely good at exposing the grinding misery, or the vulgarity and pretension, of the various social milieus with which he deals; but these are qualities which are best abstracted from the mass of populace or their physical surroundings. He can also probe brilliantly into the individual psychology of, for example, failure or jealousy. But when it comes to embodying general qualities or ideas in individuals Gissing's work sometimes falls strangely out of focus. The characters themselves are often well-realised, but it is difficult to see how he intends them to fit the theme of the novel. Luckworth Crewe, for example, who as an advertising agent stands at the centre of the cheap commercialism which *In the Year of Jubilee* so scathingly condemns, becomes an undeniably likable, even admirable, character, none the less so because of his cheerfully ruthless promotion of the ends which the novel everywhere deplores. Also, Gissing's readers must often be uncomfortably jarred by the sudden eruptions of gross prejudice which frequently occur in the novels. It is, for example, somewhat startling to hear working-class girls described in *The Odd Women* as 'mere lumps of human flesh' or to have the pretensions of an apparently fashionable assembly in *In the Year of Jubilee* exposed by the fact that the vulgar guests smell. And his attitudes to women are particularly hard to pin down, despite the fact that in his personal writings he gives the impression of being a fairly firm advocate of emancipation. He believed as staunchly as Meredith in education as the universal cure, and in a letter to his friend Eduard Bertz he explained why:

> My demand for female 'equality' simply means that I am convinced there will be no social peace until women are intellectually trained very much as men are. More than half the misery of life is due to the ignorance and childishness of women. The average woman pretty closely resembles, in all intellectual considerations, the average male *idiot* – I speak medically. That state of things is traceable to the lack of education, in all senses of the word. . . . I am driven frantic by the crass imbecility of the typical woman. That type must disappear, or at all events become altogether subordinate. And I believe that the only way of effecting this is to go through a period of what many people will call sexual anarchy.[19]

This suggests a large measure of contempt for the conventional woman slightly sweetened by hope for the future, a hope which he expressed most strongly in *The Odd Women*. It is notable, though, that when confronted by an intelligent and articulate woman somewhat after his own model, Gissing immediately fell back into the pose of sourly critical assessor of feminine charm. A wholly characteristic entry in his diary records his attendance at a feminist meeting:

> Went to the Salle des Conférences, 39 Boulevard des Capucines, at 8 o'clock and heard Louise Michel on 'Le Rôle des Femmes dans L'Humanité'. I had expected to see a face with more refinement in it; she looks painfully like a fishwife. Dressed with excessive plainness in black and wearing an ugly bonnet. [20]

Of her capacities as a speaker he observes merely that she 'showed much fluency, of course, and signs of intellect'. A face like a fishwife, it appears, overrides all the advantages of education.

We find much the same veering of conviction in Gissing's novels. His work of the nineties seems to be casting round rather wildly in an attempt to pursue some profitable line on modern womanhood and fails conspicuously to identify a consistent ideal. Janel Moxey alone, who appears fleetingly in *Born in Exile* (1892), seems to merit unequivocal support as a New Woman. A qualified doctor, and consciously independent, she has 'that peculiar fragrance of modern womanhood, refreshing, inspiriting, which is so entirely different from the merely feminine perfume, however exquisite'. Education and independence here enhance femininity: more often, emancipation corrupts natural sexuality. Sidwell Warricombe and Marcella Moxey, in the same novel, are respectively asexual and coldly intolerant. In *Denzil Quarrier* (1892) we have Mrs Wade, the ferocious feminist who drives the hero's fluttering little wife to suicide, and in *The Emancipated* (1890) Miriam Baske, grappling painfully with inflexible religious pride and puritan prejudice. All are highly intelligent women with strong views on their own emancipation, but all are found wanting in feminine terms. By contrast, women who do display the conventional qualities of femininity – qualities which themselves are frequently condemned by Gissing – often earn further black marks when they achieve a surface gloss of emancipation. Thus Amy Reardon in *New Grub Street*(1891) quotes Spencer and speaks sturdily in favour of freer divorce, but these signs of intellectual advance are merely correlatives of her general superficiality: 'Anything that savoured of newness and boldness in philosophic thought had a charm for her palate. . . . She was becoming a typical woman of the time'. Interestingly, the two major novels which Gissing produced during the New Woman boom develop these character types as central figures. In *The Odd Women* we have Rhoda Nunn, at first so fiercely feminist that she appears almost sexless, and in *In the Year of Jubilee* Nancy Lord, whose instinctive feminine refinement is cheapened and made vulgar by her slick modern education and modish ideas about women's position.

Despite the fact that Gissing recorded it as having been 'scribbled in six weeks', *The Odd Women* (1893) is a complex and highly structured novel. It is complex – or perhaps complicated – in its attempt to integrate its various thematic strands and numerous characters, and in structure it achieves some neat correspondences and contrasts. However, the novel seems to illustrate some of Gissing's recurrent problems: its general thrust does not always seem well supported by the individuals who embody it. There are frequent muddles; the characters' particular attributes often rub uncomfortably against their general polemical functions, and there appears to be a strong thematic undertow which pulls curiously against the ostensible flow of the novel's purpose.

The main female characters are 'odd' primarily in the sense of being conventionally superfluous; they are examples of the half-million or so women who, merely by virtue of the fact that they exceed the male population, are statistically damned to spinster-hood. Many of them are odd, too, in the more usual sense of the word, a condition which is exacerbated by the difficulties to which, in their unmarried and impoverished state, they are inevitably subjected. Two alternatives to this combination of oddness are offered: the first, and more practical and forward-looking, is that of organised work-schemes, represented by Miss Barfoot's establishment which trains young women in typing and clerical skills, and stiffens their resolve with rousing orations on the condition of women; the second, for most a forlorn hope, is marriage at any price. *The Odd Women* of course throws its weight behind the first, but, perhaps because the enterprise is so obviously worthy and needed, is disappointingly vague about the actual details of its working. Miss Barfoot's training school stands firm at the centre of the novel as a beacon of enlightenment and resource, beckoning the poor and misguided and generously dispensing the warmth of its idealism, but never revealing its inner mechanisms. By contrast the second alternative, marriage, is probed minutely, on one level through the detailed analysis of contrasting couples, and on another by the continual barrage of damning evidence from minor characters. The training scheme survives as a slightly nebulous ideal; marriage, attacked on all sides and from almost every point of view, naturally falls apart, but in muddle and confusion rather than from a clean polemical cut.

The odd women are represented mainly by the hapless Madden sisters. The novel opens with a discussion of women's role in money-matters, Dr Madden explaining to his eldest daughter that he is about to insure his life because 'nothing upsets me more than the sight of those poor homes where wife and children are obliged to talk from morning to night of how the sorry earnings shall be laid out. No, no; women, old or young, should never have to think about money'. The rest of the novel is to show them doing little else: Dr Madden dies before his intention is fulfilled and his willing but talentless daughters are cast upon a world which has little to offer in the way of help or hope. Though the Madden girls' numbers are soon reduced, in a few pitiless asides, from six to three (Isabel, for example, works herself into 'brain trouble' and 'melancholia', and is taken in by a 'charitable institution' where 'at two-and-twenty, the poor hard-featured girl drowned herself in a bath') their tiny inheritance is still insufficient to support them. The elder girls, Alice and Virginia, drift hopelessly from one badly-paid post to another, cheering themselves occasionally with the thought that their younger sister Monica, being blessed with good looks, may eventually escape the grind: 'She must marry; of course she must marry! Her sisters gladdened in the thought'. It is interesting to note, though, that in the early part of the novel Gissing seems to recognise the Maddens as something of an anachronism in being poor and untrained: they are, it seems, competing for jobs with highly qualified professionals. 'There is so little choice for people like myself', moans Alice. 'Certificates, even degrees, are asked for on every hand.' But this is a point which seems to be forgotten later on when Miss Barfoot's efforts in the training of odd women are presented as uniquely pioneering.

The Maddens might pin their hopes on Monica's marriage, but others are competing for her in different fields. When chance brings Virginia into contact in London with her childhood friend Rhoda Nunn a new world of female endeavour is opened to her dimly wondering eyes. The scene in which the feeble, drooping Virginia meets the briskly abrasive Rhoda is very nicely done. For Virginia 'it was the first time in her life that she had spoken with a woman daring enough to think and act for herself', and the efficacy of this independence is attested by the fact that it is also the first occasion for some time when Virginia is able to eat meat, tactfully pressed upon her by her infinitely more successful friend. Rhoda, who, having learnt shorthand, bookkeeping and commercial correspondence, 'felt [herself] worth something in the world', had gone to Miss Barfoot to train in typing and now assists her in running the school. She quickly sums up Virginia as too far gone to benefit from a typing course herself, but suggests that Monica, currently working inhuman hours in a draper's shop, is suitable material, and Alice and Virginia persuade their somewhat reluctant sister to enrol.

Miss Barfoot herself, though retaining many traditional feminine graces, is presented as a model of excellence for the modern working woman. Her training school sends out fully qualified women to compete on equal terms in masculine fields, and her speeches to the pupils are truly rousing appeals to the new spirit, more complete and convincing – perhaps because more lengthy – than anything in the popular New Woman novels:

> I am a troublesome, aggressive, revolutionary person. I want to do away with that common confusion of the words womanly and womanish, and I see very clearly that this can only be affected by an armed movement, an invasion by women of the spheres which men have always forbidden us to enter. . . .
> . . . It is very far from our wish to cause hardship to any one, but we ourselves are escaping from a hardship that has become intolerable. We are educating ourselves. There must be a new type of woman, active in every sphere of life: a new worker out in the world, a new ruler of the home. Of the old ideal virtues we can retain many, but we have to add to them those which have been thought appropriate only in men. Let a woman be gentle, but at the same time let her be strong; let her be pure of heart, but none the less wise and instructed. Because we have to set an example to the sleepy of our sex, we must carry on an active warfare – must be invaders. Whether woman is the equal of man I neither know nor care. We are not his equal in size, in weight, in muscle, and, for all I can say, we may have less power of brain. That has nothing to do with it. Enough for us to know that our natural growth has been stunted. The mass of women have always been paltry creatures, and their paltriness has proved a curse to men. So, if you like to put it this way, we are working for the advantage of men as well as for our own. Let the responsibility for disorder rest on those who have made us despise our old selves. At any

cost – at any cost – we will free ourselves from the heritage of weakness and contempt. (ch. 13)

Miss Barfoot combines some of the current New Woman qualities – the general militancy, the idea that a woman's 'purity' should be based on knowledge and education – with some notions more peculiar to Gissing. He would certainly endorse the sentiment that 'the mass of women have always been paltry creatures', and felt very strongly that this had been more of a curse to men – particularly himself – than to women. The idea that the New Women are a blessing to men is one which, as we shall see, runs throughout the novel. In other passages too we learn things about Miss Barfoot's establishment which may disquiet the reader but which clearly have Gissing's support. Rhoda tells Virginia that 'Miss Barfoot hasn't much interest in the lower classes', a point which is expanded later when Mrs Smallbrook, a philanthropist who, Gissing tells us, 'could only be considered a bore', tackles Miss Barfoot on her attitude towards working-class women. 'But surely you don't limit your humanity . . . by the artificial divisions of society?' she asks, to which Miss Barfoot 'good-humouredly' replies 'In the uneducated classes I have no interest whatever'. The fact that these women are just as likely to be 'odd' as the conventionally-educated but empty-headed Madden sisters seems to disturb neither Miss Barfoot nor Gissing.

Still, there is always the alternative of marriage, a temptation which is held out, in contrasting ways, to both Rhoda and Monica. To Rhoda it comes through Miss Barfoot's suave young cousin Everard, who begins by savouring the challenge to his masculine charm of a self-contained, almost sexless, woman, and ends by falling genuinely in love, and to Monica through the lonely middle-aged bachelor Widdowson, who is steeped in Ruskin's views on women and tries to make the miserable Monica conform to his impossible ideal. Both relationships fail, though for very different reasons, and beneath the two detailed investigations of the couples' problems we have a continual chorus of anti-marriage lament. Although Rhoda, at the beginning of the novel stridently anti-marriage, maintains that 'the vast majority of women lead a vain and miserable life just because they *do* marry', the actual evidence we are given strongly supports Miss Barfoot's assertion that the paltriness of women has proved a curse to men. Everard regales Miss Barfoot and Rhoda with horror stories about his friends' marriages;

one was married to a woman incapable of understanding a joke, another to a wife who would talk about nothing but her servants. The first unfortunate man is eventually confined to a lunatic asylum, the second is last seen 'worn to skin and bone' in Alexandria, 'wandering round the shores of the Mediterranean like an uneasy spirit'. The general stupidity of women, we gather, has a lot to answer for. Nor is the Barfoot family exempt. Examples closer to home are given through the experiences of Everard's father, hampered by an early marriage of which he always spoke 'bitterly', and his brother Tom, whose wife's appalling selfishness is literally the death of him. 'When one thinks how often a woman is a clog upon a man's ambition, no wonder they regard us as they do', comments Miss Barfoot, sweetly sympathetic. Later, however, particularly through Monica, we learn that it is possible for women to suffer too. Monica's wedding is described in terms of gloom worthy of Hardy:

> Depression was manifest on every countenance. . . . For an hour before going to the church, Monica had cried and seemed unutterably doleful; she had not slept for two nights; her face was ghastly . . .
>
> There was breakfast, more dismal fooling than even this species of fooling is wont to be. Mr Newdick, trembling and bloodless, proposed Monica's health; Widdowson, stern and dark as ever, gloomily responded; and then, *that* was happily over. (ch. 12)

It is notable, though, that while Everard's friends and relations are, apart from their initial stupidity in selecting their mates, entirely blameless in the marital breakdowns, the novel contains no example of a wife as wholly innocent victim. For Gissing, the marriage odds are, despite some obvious feminist convictions, weighted more against men than women.

This tug of sympathies is manifest in Gissing's treatment of Monica's marriage. Widdowson picks her up, in the politest possible way, on a park bench, and from this unpromising start the relationship goes almost steadily downhill. From the beginning Monica regards Widdowson personally as better than nothing, and marriage in general as a preferable state to either shop assistant or trainee typist. 'As things went in the marriage war, she might esteem herself a most fortunate young woman.' Despite the fact that, in their terms, Monica counts as educated and is moreover clearly making a bad match, Miss Barfoot and Rhoda agree that she is doing the right thing and rather callously consign her to the dustheap of marriage. She does, though, get a stern warning from her friend Mildred:

> I think you're going to marry with altogether wrong ideas. I think you'll do an injustice to Mr Widdowson. You will marry him for a comfortable home – that's what it amounts to. And you'll repent it bitterly some day – you'll repent. (ch. 11)

All this is amply justified by events. In particular, despite his undoubted cruelties and absurd notions about women, the idea that Widdowson is a victim of injustice is one which Gissing allows repeatedly to bob up and break the smooth surface of sympathy for Monica. In a sense, of course, it is quite true that in marrying without love Monica is being unfair, though Widdowson is so determinedly infatuated that he never suspects the obvious, and the whole odd woman theme suggests that marriage is generally regarded as the best means for a woman to earn a living rather than as a sentimental ideal. But after the marriage it is undoubtedly Widdowson who makes life intolerable for Monica through the exercise of his peculiarly exaggerated male prejudices. 'He was unconsciously the most complete despot, a monument of male autocracy. Never had it occurred to Widdowson that a wife remains an individual, with rights and obligations independent of her wifely condition.' Widdowson becomes increasingly morose and suspicious, resenting the slightest show of independence on Monica's part and eventually going to the lengths of shadowing her on her rare excursions from the marital home. He responds to her very reasonable contention that housework does not provide full or satisfying occupation for her with the observation that it is 'not only . . . your duty, dear, but your privilege', and gradually Monica begins to recall her Barfoot training and argue tentatively for equality:

> 'I don't think, Edmund, there's much real difference between men and women. That is, there wouldn't be, if women had fair treatment.'
> 'Not much difference? Oh, come; you are talking nonsense. There's as much difference between their minds as between their bodies. They are made for entirely different duties.'

Monica sighed.
'Oh, that word Duty!' (ch. 16)

Clearly Monica has reason and justice on her side, and also, as
Gissing points out, shows considerable courage in forcing her
husband into such arguments. 'A much older woman might have
envied her steadfast yet quite rational assertion of the right to live a
life of her own apart from that imposed upon her by the duties of
wedlock', he comments. But as often happens in this part of the
novel, the strongest pleas in favour of women are qualified by some
evidence of their weakness or unreliability. Monica is not being
totally honest. This discussion has been preceded by a week in
which she has indulged Widdowson's every whim and pretended to
return his devotion in full. His blind love has trapped him into
responding to an argument which actually threatens its foundations. 'During the past week [Monica] had conducted herself so as
to smooth the way for this very discussion,' says Gissing, adding
darkly, 'unsuspecting husband!'.

Monica has been playing a woman's game, using feminine wiles
to soften up her husband, and once started on this course she quickly
extends it into more dangerous areas. She begins to flirt with the
attractive, but superficial and cowardly Bevis, and from here on she
ceases to be able to confront Widdowson with abstract justice. Her
desire for greater freedom is now for the freedom to deceive him
with another man, and their roles begin to shift. Widdowson's
jealousies and fears are now fully justified; and he even proves
himself capable of rationality and generous indulgence in his
sentiments towards her:

> He would endeavour to win her respect by respecting the freedom
> she claimed. His recent suspicions of her were monstrous. If she
> knew them, how her soul would revolt from him! . . .
>   They were bound to each other for life, and their wisdom lay in
> mutual toleration, the constant endeavour to understand each
> other aright – not in fierce restraint of each other's mental liberty.
> How many marriages were anything more than mutual for-
> bearance? Perhaps there ought not to be such a thing as enforced
> permanence of marriage. . . . Perhaps, some day, marriage
> would be dissoluble at the will of either party to it. Perhaps the
> man who sought to hold a woman when she no longer loved him
> would be regarded with contempt and condemnation. (ch. 23)

This enlightenment does not last long – Widdowson soon returns from 'the realms of reason . . . to the safe sphere of the commonplace' – but his reflections are at once essential to the novel's argument on marriage and symptomatic of the sort of confusions Gissing gets into. Widdowson's excursion into what Gissing praises as the 'realms of reason' also, we note, opens him to the most savage irony. While Widdowson is reflecting that his recent suspicions of Monica are 'monstrous' she is at that very moment in Bevis's flat asking him to take her away to France. Moreover, Widdowson's advanced thoughts are, significantly, the most sustained plea for freer divorce which the novel contains. Gissing is perhaps suggesting the point that bitter experience of marriage can force the most reactionary of men into enlightened thought, but it is notable that he has to pull Widdowson sharply back into conformity in order to re-establish sympathy for Monica. Widdowson's 'excursion into the realms of reason' is a brief sortie out of character, necessary to argue points that Gissing wants to make, but not well integrated to the situation. It is right in the abstract for a man to decide that gross suspicions of a wife are monstrous, but in the particular instance they are absolutely correct. The general arguments are not properly embodied in their specific illustrations.

Monica dies, totally estranged from her husband, in childbirth, her tragedy brought about primarily but not entirely by the extreme bigotry of her husband. Meanwhile, though, Rhoda and Everard are trying to establish their relationship along totally contrasting lines as a model of freedom and equality. At the beginning of the novel Rhoda, despite her admirable independence, is portrayed as intolerant and over-harsh in her feminist militancy. The fact that she has never been loved, everybody privately agrees, is the root of the problem, an omission which she too feels sharply: 'Secretly she deemed it a hard thing never to have known that common triumph of her sex'. Everard is fascinated by her hard exterior, wishing to probe to a soft core of feminine responsiveness, and Rhoda is, it seems, titillated by Everard's man-of-the-world air and sophisticated masculinity: 'Barfoot interested her, and not the less because of his evil reputation. . . . She could not but regard him with sexual curiosity'. However, there seems to be a certain confusion in the presentation of Everard. Sometimes he appears as a genuine advanced thinker, professing sympathy with his cousin's enterprise and arguing fluently in favour of free love.

There are times, too when he seems honestly to appreciate Rhoda as a New Woman, a term which he himself applies to her:

> He enjoyed her air of equality; she sat down with him as a male acquaintance might have done, and he felt sure that her behaviour would be the same under any circumstances. He delighted in her frankness of speech; it was doubtful whether she regarded any subject as improper for discussion between mature and serious people. (ch. 10)

But often he appears merely as a smooth deceiver, his advanced thought nothing more than a bait to catch New Women. His relationship with Rhoda quickly degenerates into a crude power struggle. Everard professes belief in free love and states unequivocally that 'my own ideal of marriage involves perfect freedom on both sides', but his attitude towards Rhoda is more that of the oppressively dominant male. Both Everard and Rhoda are theoretically committed to the principle of equality, but neither is prepared to practise it. Rhoda wants to prove her power by making Everard propose marriage – 'he would plead with her to become his legal wife', 'she had the sense of exultation, of triumph' – after which she would consent to free union, and Everard wants to make Rhoda agree to free union – 'he was satisfied with nothing short of unconditional surrender', 'he . . . desired to see her in complete subjugation to him' – after which he would consent to marriage. Thus the whole idea of free love is debased into a bargaining point. Their relationship founders on the question, but in a wholly artificial way. What one might expect, in a novel dedicated to an investigation of women and marriage, to be a central thematic concept turns out merely to be a crude plot device for impeding the path of love. Free love is chosen, obviously, for its associations with modernism and the New Woman, but there is remarkably little examination of what it actually means. Neither Everard nor Rhoda really explain their reasons for rejecting or advocating it, or enunciate its advantage over marriage or its social implications.

However, the breaking of this relationship causes little lasting misery. Gissing sticks with commendable resolve to his conception of Rhoda as essentially a career woman, and moreover succeeds remarkably well in persuading his readers that work is in no sense a poor substitute for love. Even before the break, Rhoda is feeling doubts about how well marriage will compare with her previous working life:

What was her life to be? At first they would travel together; but
before long it might be necessary to have a settled home, and
what then would be her social position, her duties and pleasures?
Housekeeping, mere domesticities, could never occupy her for
more than the smallest possible part of each day. Having lost one
purpose in life, dignified, absorbing, likely to extend its sphere as
time went on, what other could she hope to substitute for it? (ch.
26)

Rhoda's relationship with Everard is useful in reassuring her that
work is, for women, a genuine alternative to marriage; she is an odd
woman by choice, not necessity.

Everard and Rhoda are not merely contrasts to Widdowson and
Monica; the two couples are also neatly linked by the plot. Because
Everard occupies a flat in the same building as Bevis, both Rhoda
and Widdowson are led to believe that Monica's illicit visits are in
fact to him. And this mistake pinpoints the strong sub-theme of the
novel, that of jealousy. The last part of *The Odd Women* is written
largely as a fairly standard love story, gratuitously multiplying
confusions in order to entangle the four lovers in a web of deceit and
misunderstanding, with jealousy as the destructive emotion. Both
Widdowson and Rhoda are tormented by it, their suspicions neatly
converging on the same object; and as background to the two main
sufferers we have several minor victims. Miss Barfoot, we learn, had
as a young girl been in love with Everard, and her relationship with
Rhoda is thus temporarily poisoned when she sees her cousin falling
in love with her. We also have the unfortunate Miss Eade, who pops
up from time to time with vicious accusations against Monica of
supposedly having stolen her young man and is last seen, powdered
and painted, soliciting on a railway station. Corroding jealousy is an
emotion which permeates the novel, but which seems to have little
to do with the main theme; indeed with Rhoda it seems badly to
shake the case for regarding her relationship with Everard as a
softening and humanising influence. It provides another example of
the muddling of intent which blurs this novel's effect. Still, *The Odd
Women* contains many fine things: the portrayal of the elder
Madden sisters, with Virginia darting furtively into railway
refreshment rooms for a tot of brandy, or plain, sallow Alice
stumping with stolid courage from one disappointment to the next,
is striking without being grotesque, sympathetic without being
mawkish. And despite the lapses of consistency and the occasional

polemical hiatus, the New Woman theme is handled with sensitivity and suggests genuine involvement in the woman's cause.

It is , then, particularly surprising to find Gissing producing, the following year, a novel which takes such a diametrically opposed line on women and marriage. *In the Year of Jubilee* (1894) contains a blueprint for happy wedlock which seems to deny all the ideals of equality put forward in *The Odd Women*. The novel is, as Gissing said, a 'picture of certain detestable phases of modern life'[21] and in places reaches a pitch of loathing remarkable even for him. Particularly savage is the 'satire on sham education' which, though directed partly at ignorant and pretentious young men, is primarily aimed at the female characters. Gissing may have been firmly in favour of education for women, but of an education very different from anything that was actually offered; here the words 'course' or 'examination' make him almost hysterical in his abuse. This sort of education, it appears, leads either to intellectual aridity and madness, or, more usually, to excesses of vulgarity. Mr Lord, father of the heroine Nancy, is clearly speaking for Gissing in his diatribe against modern womanhood:

> Wherever you look now-a-days there's sham and rottenness; but the most worthless creature living is one of these trashy, flashy, girls, – the kind of girl you see everywhere, high and low, – calling themselves 'ladies', – thinking themselves too good for any honest, womanly work. Town and country, it's all the same. They're educated; oh yes, they're educated! What sort of wives do they make, with their education? What sort of mothers are they? Before long, there'll be no such thing as a home. They don't know what the word means. They'd like to live in hotels, and trollop about the streets day and night . . . It is astounding to me that they don't get their necks wrung. (Part I, ch. 5)

As examples of this we have the French sisters, 'the product of sham education and mock refinement grafted upon a stock of robust vulgarity'. Through them Gissing pours out all his hatred of cheap modernity. In his portrayal of the eldest sister, Ada, he appears to be drawing on his own wretched experiences with Edith Underwood; Ada's screaming matches with the servants, her contempt for her long-suffering husband and cruel neglect of her child all correspond with accounts of Edith. The youngest girl, Fanny, wooed by the foolishly doting Horace Lord, is in Gissing's eyes little better than a prostitute. Loud-mouthed and idiotically good-humoured, her brash composure when Horace draws her lovingly onto his knee suggests to Gissing that 'no second year graduate of the pavement could have preserved a greater equanimity'. And when at one point the sisters are seen rolling on the floor in a vicious fight Gissing is able finally to give full vent to his rage and loathing:

> Now indeed the last trace of veneer was gone, the last rag of pseudo-civilisation was rent off these young women; in physical conflict, vilifying each other like the female spawn of White-chapel, they revealed themselves as born – raw material which the mill of education is supposed to convert into middle-class ladyhood. (Part IV, ch. 5)

But though the middle sister, Beatrice, is included in this, she is, as we shall see, a different and rather more interesting case.

At opposite ends of the shamly educated spectrum are Jessica Morgan, 'a dolorous image of frustrate sex', who spends most of the novel vainly cramming for exams and ends half-crazed with overwork and jealousy, and the heroine, Nancy Lord. Though superficially educated in the same way as Jessica and the French sisters, Nancy has a measure of instinctive refinement which raises her above the others and allows her in the end to illustrate what one can only assume is Gissing's new ideal of womanhood. At the beginning of the novel she displays what at first looks like an admirably modern desire for independence. She chafes against her father's old-fashioned ideals of ladylike behaviour, and signals her dissatisfaction with his insistence on chaperonage by sallying forth alone into the midst of the jubilee-night crowds. But Gissing is sternly disapproving of her delight in freedom; her face, he says, shows 'vulgar abandonment' and her 'emotions differed little from those of any shop-girl let loose'. She is poised, then, between sinking to the French level or being raised to something more valuable, and when she meets one of Gissing's smooth young men, Lionel Tarrant, it seems that her path will be upward. At first Tarrant is merely amused by this rawly pretentious girl from the suburbs, but soon he becomes more deeply involved. In a scene very reminiscent of *Tess of the D'Urbervilles* he seduces her, though unlike Tess she is an obviously willing victim. Tarrant then shows himself to have some oddly old-fashioned notions of honour and marries her im-mediately, but because of some rather creaky machinations with her father's will the marriage has to be kept secret and the two live apart. She becomes pregnant, and Tarrant coolly takes himself off to the Bahamas to make his fortune.

It is curiously difficult to see how Gissing's sympathies are divided. At first it seems almost impossible to believe that he can really be giving his approval to Tarrant in actions which appear so blatantly unfair, and indeed Nancy is sometimes allowed to feel righteously ill-used. However, even before he leaves for the Bahamas Tarrant is lecturing Nancy on the merits of separate living, and there is nothing to suggest that Gissing disagrees with him:

> I look at it in this way. We ought to regard ourselves as married people living under exceptionally favourable circumstances. One has to bear in mind the brutal fact that man and wife, as a rule, see a great deal too much of each other – thence most of the ills of married life: squabblings, small or great disgusts. . . . People get to think themselves victims of incompatibility, when they are merely suffering from a foolish custom – the habit of being perpetually together. In fact, it's an immoral custom. . . . The common practice of man and wife occupying the same room is monstrous, gross; it's astounding that women of any sensitiveness can endure it. (Part III, ch. 6)

'I can agree with all that', says Nancy, but still, to Tarrant's intense irritation, shows signs of sadness at his impending departure. Gissing seems to allow that Tarrant is being a little heartless in his desertion of Nancy, but continually insists that she should not clog his path with lachrymose sentiment. When she too comes to an understanding of this, she is rewarded with a resurgence of Tarrant's love. 'I am independent of you', she says, 'I shall love you just as little as possible – and how little that will be, perhaps I had better not tell you', to which he sighs out 'you look very beautiful today'. It almost turns into an object lesson in how to keep your man.

The idea that a woman's independence is a desirable thing – desirable, that is, in that it frees a man from annoying and unnecessary demands on his attention – is developed in the rest of the novel. Nancy is left in a most difficult position. Because her marriage has to be kept secret, she cannot openly acknowledge her child. It is born in secrecy and bundled off as quickly as possible to foster parents, but when Beatrice French's pryings unearth the fact of its existence Nancy has to pretend to be an unmarried mother and accept the shame involved. But Gissing sticks immovably to his notion that Nancy is a most fortunate young woman, and forces her to feel the same way:

> Strangely as it seemed to her, she grew conscious of a personal freedom not unlike what she had vainly desired in the days of petulant girlhood; the sense came only at moments, but was real and precious; under its influence she forgot everything abnormal in her situation, and – though without recognising this sig- nificance – knew the exultation of a woman who has justified her being. (Part IV, ch. 7)

Nancy has justified her being, apparently, in having a child she hardly sees and a husband on the other side of the world. She is one of the odd mixes which 'advanced' writers of the nineties often produced, New Woman in her desire for 'personal freedom' old- fashioned male ideal in achieving this through maternity and wifehood, however unconventional their manifestations. When Tarrant falls from grace, even in Gissing's eyes, by ceasing to write to her, Nancy strikes out on a course which looks more fashionably feminist. Abandoning all hope of marital happiness, she decides to try for fulfilment through work and takes a job in Beatrice's dressmaking business. But this, we find, is contrived simply as a black mark against Tarrant. It is Nancy who has the right idea, and Tarrant's neglect which has pushed her off the correct path:

> The word 'home' grew very sweet to her ears. A man, she said to herself, may go forth and find his work, his pleasure, in the highways: but is not a woman's place under the sheltering roof? What right had a mother to be seeking abroad for tasks and duties? Task enough, duty obvious, in the tending of her child. Had she but a little country cottage, with needs assured, and her baby cradled beside her, she would ask no more. (Part V, ch. 1)

It is a good thing that this is what she wants, because, with the minor substitution of a surburban semi for a country cottage, it is what she gets. When Tarrant returns to England he is met with an understandably cool reception: 'I am *not* your wife! You married me against your will, and shook me off as soon as possible. I won't be bound to you; I shall act as a free woman'. And although this stirring New Woman stuff is presented initially as a sympathetic indulgence of Nancy's feelings of rejection, Gissing quickly turns it to the man's advantage. Tarrant makes some gestures in the direction of remorse, and then sets about building a life which will exploit Nancy's professed desire for independence in a way most convenient to himself. Once again, female independence is shown to benefit the man. Nancy may wish to settle down in domestic harmony with the newly loving Tarrant, but he insists that she should stick to her resolve and live apart from him: 'Even if you were willing, it would be a mistake for us to live together. For one thing, I couldn't work under such conditions'. It is an eminently sensible arrangement, Gissing maintains; Tarrant is able to go off to glittering dinner parties unencumbered by a wife, and can get on with his work without having to worry about his family: 'I often think in a troubled way about you; but you are out of my sight, and that enables me to keep you out of mind'. Nancy's acquiescence in this extraordinary arrangement is indicated by her calm pleasure when Tarrant favours her with a visit and the equanimity – even polite interest – with which she listens to his descriptions of the brilliant and beautiful women he has met. Here is one type of relationship, Gissing proudly suggests, which will never be sullied by jealousy and which will not drive a long-suffering husband mad. 'There is not one wife in fifty thousand who retains her husband's love after the first year of marriage', says Tarrant, but Gissing has found a way for Nancy to do it. When Tarrant finally makes it clear that he will not live with her in the foreseeable future and asks grumblingly 'You are still dissatisfied?' Gissing triumphantly unveils Nancy as every man's ideal wife: 'She looked up, and commanded her features to the expression which makes whatever woman lovely – that of rational acquiescence'. Widdowson would have been delighted.

Clearly this novel, though making a woman the central character, is written with a man's interests in mind. Free wives make free husbands and the important work of the world – childbearing for women, intellectual exercise for men – will be done all the better. But Gissing's eye for modern movements, though here particularly jaundiced, was always acute, and in the portrayal of Beatrice French and her relationship with Nancy we get some fascinating insights into the way he saw the new women developing. Beatrice is like Luckworth Crewe in representing all the cheapness and vulgarity of the modern business world, but at the same time displaying an irreverent enthusiasm and dynamic energy which makes them, almost against Gissing's will, interesting and even admirable characters. She is the type of 'New Woman' beloved by the popular press, unprincipled, unfeminine and excitingly dangerous. A successful business woman who is addressed affectionately by her male colleagues as 'old chap', she lives alone in a flat and has arranged her life along eminently independent lines. When Nancy drops in unexpectedly she is given

> a very satisfying meal . . . not badly cooked, as cooking is understood in Brixton, and served with more of ceremony than the guest had expected. Fried scallops, rump steak smothered in onions, an apple tart, and very sound Stilton cheese. Such fare testified to the virile qualities of Beatrice's mind; she was above the feminine folly of neglecting honest victuals. Moreover, there appeared two wines, sherry and claret. (Part V, ch. 4)

After dinner Beatrice settles down to smoke – 'it's expected of a sensible woman nowadays' – and to savour one of her excellent wines. When she shows Nancy round the flat, she apologises for the smallness of the bedroom and adds 'archly' 'but I sleep single'. It develops into a scene of striking modernity, with Nancy and Beatrice, the one a supposedly unmarried mother, the other a successful career woman, sitting comfortably over wine and cigarettes discussing their lives and loves. Despite the general antifeminist line of the novel, this is very much a New Woman situation, and it is one of the things Gissing could always do very well. Unlike either Hardy or Meredith, he is superbly good at portraying women simply as people, without any suggestion of interest or involvement in their specifically feminine qualities. It is a point which he expressed most succinctly through Constance Bride in *Our Friend the Charlatan* (1901): 'I hate talk about *women*. We've had enough of it; it has become a nuisance – a cant, like any other. A woman is a human being, not a separate species'.

However, *In the Year of Jubilee* has only brief flashes of this detachment. It is on the whole an uneasy combination of some modern attitudes to women with an ill-disguised hankering after the old ideals, and in his next major novel, *The Whirlpool* (1897),this descent from the feminism of *The Odd Women* is even more apparent. Here Gissing seems to come into the open with his contempt for modern womanhood and his despair about marriage. After reading the novel, Eduard Bertz wrote to Gissing: 'It is remarkable how greatly you are inclined to pessimism in your delineation of women and marriage: that makes a great difference from your earlier books; your realism is much more pronounced than formerly'.[22] And the idea that a realistic view of women and marriage necessarily entailed pessimism is one which permeates the novel, spreading a pall of weary Hardyesque gloom over its pages. 'Marriage rarely means happiness, either for men or women; if it be not too grievous to be borne, one must thank the fates and take courage', we are told. The middle-aged hero, Harvey Rolfe, had, Gissing informs us, 'run through follies innumerable, but from the supreme folly of hampering himself by marriage, a merciful fate had guarded him'. But when he meets a self-consciously posturing New Woman, Alma Fotheringham, his guardian angel deserts him and he embarks on the miserable path of the married man. By 1897, it seems, the New Woman had become a fashionable and essentially respectable society figure, and Alma uses her pose of emancipation to fascinate and enslave the innocent Rolfe. It all ends in misery and disillusion, of course – 'Harvey did but share the common lot of men married; he recognised the fact, and was too wise to complain of it, even in his own mind'. But the novel does contain one example of domestic bliss in the Morton family, presided over by a sort of Victorian earth-mother. Mrs Morton

> conceived her duty as wife and mother after the old fashion, and was so fortunate as to find no obstacle in the circumstances. . . . Four children she had borne . . . and it seemed to her no merit that in these little ones she saw the end and reason of her being. Into her pure and healthy mind had never entered a thought of conflict with motherhood. Her breasts were the fountains of life; her babies clung to them, and grew large of limb. From her they learnt to speak; from her they learnt the names of trees and flowers and all things beautiful around them; learnt too, less by precept than from fair example, the sweetness and sincerity wherewith such mothers, and such alone, can endow their offspring. (Part III, ch. 1)

Nothing more cloyingly conventional could be imagined.

This does not stand as Gissing's final word on women. His later novels, though less interesting in most respects than his other work, contain scattered references to female emancipation and revolutionary ideas about marriage but never explore them in much detail.

No constant view of women emerges from the body of his work: he swings between the extremes of Rhoda Nunn and Mrs Morton without finding any satisfactory resting place. It is always dangerous to extrapolate too freely from an author's life to his work, but it is perhaps not difficult to understand how Gissing's wretched experiences with Nell and Edith could make him see advantages in the Lionel Tarrant model of marriage which are less apparent to the average reader. One can see also the temptation to wallow nostalgically in the old domestic ideals. But his abrupt switches of direction on the woman question seem symptomatic of much that is puzzling in his work: he is opinionated without having consistent views; aggressive without always identifying his target.

Like Hardy and Meredith, Gissing reached his height of feminist conviction during the years of the New Woman novel's popularity. None of the three can be convicted simply of writing to catch the fashionable conscience, since all had previously demonstrated their interest in some of the New Woman's ideas, but that all three were encouraged, perhaps sharpened, by the popular debate cannot be in doubt. To some extent Gissing's ability to draw a woman as 'a human being, not a separate species' sets him apart from the other two. His range in female characterisation is wider than Hardy's or Meredith's, though he is correspondingly more inconsistent in conviction than either. But though utterly opposed to Meredith in mood, he is not so remote in opinion. Two constants emerge from Gissing's portrayal of women which run steadily through Meredith's work: both deplored shallowness in women and both at the same time demanded an innate femininity. Meredith made his women courageous, independent, educated and unquestionably refined. Gissing, we note, insists that Rhoda Nunn prove her femininity by loving before she is released with all the credentials to do noble work, and that Nancy Lord spice her domestic idyll with '*rational* acquiescence' and an appreciation of her husband's intellect. But the fact that conventional 'femininity' sometimes implied shallowness obviously perplexed Gissing far more than Meredith. Meredith was always clear about what he wanted from women and produced a reasonably attractive, though limited, model. Gissing, searching as desperately in art as in life, never quite reconciled his ideals.

Conclusion

In *The Wife of Sir Isaac Harman*, written in 1914, H. G. Wells offers some parenthetical observations on the decline of English fiction into what he saw as bland politeness. 'The last wild idea', he reflects, '. . . had been hunted down and killed in the mobbing of *The Woman Who Did*.' Certainly Grant Allen's novel brought a virtual end to the popular New Woman fiction, and those major authors who had, in various ways, lent support to the movement closed their careers in novel-writing at much the same time. Hardy never produced another novel after *Jude the Obscure*; though Meredith lived until 1909, his fictional output ended, in the same year as Hardy's, with *The Amazing Marriage*; and Gissing, while continuing to write until his death in 1903, produced little of importance after 1897 with *The Whirlpool*. The New Woman heroine did not outlast the Victorian age. A new reign and a new century arriving at the same time gave a powerful impression of fresh starts and different concerns. In the year of Gissing's death, Mrs Emmeline Pankhurst and her daughters founded the Women's Social and Political Union; for women, it seemed, the anti-marriage era was at an end, and the period of the suffragette beginning.

An odd complacency crept into discussions of the woman question. Ellen Key, for example, felt able in 1912 to pronounce the employment battles as good as won: 'That a dwelling was denied to the first woman physician because her profession was considered "improper" for a woman, sounds now like a fable. Everywhere now are women nurses, teachers of gymnastics, dentists, apothecaries, and midwives'.[1] As early as 1902, an article on 'The New Woman' was clearly regarding her major campaigns as honourably concluded: 'In few respects has mankind made a greater advance than in the position of women – legal, social and educational. From the darkness of ignorance and servitude woman has passed into the open light of equal freedom'.[2] The alarming creature who, when providing the central character in fiction a decade earlier, was regarded as the dangerous figment of a diseased imagination, is now, we rather surprisingly learn, an established fact of the social scene, someone who must moreover be gently cajoled into a return to domestic duty. The New Woman is cautioned to

> bear in mind that in becoming a brilliant mathematician, a sharp critic, a faultless grammarian, she may do so at the expense of that ready sympathy, modesty, noble self-control, gentleness, personal tact and temper, so essential for the best type of womanhood and the most exalted standards of female excellence.[3]

Though the old fears remain, the tone in which they are expressed has changed from strident abuse to tactful reservation; critics of the New Woman now feel themselves to be dealing with an actual person rather than a projected ideal and adjust their tactics accordingly. In an article on 'The Threatened Re-Subjection of Women', reflecting a major change in its very title, Lucas Malet wonders despairingly 'by what form of bribery, by what appeal to the magic of hereditary instinct, you can charm the New Woman – sexless, homeless, unmaternal as she increasingly is – back to the store-closet and the nursery'.[4] That she should be supposed to have effected such a complete escape is, in itself, remarkable.

This shift in attitude is widely reflected in the fiction of the pre-First World War period. Novelists with a professionally keen eye for modern movements – E. F. Benson, E.V. Lucas, H. G. Wells – take the emancipated woman as a representative figure of the age, and, accepting Lucas Malet's challenge, show time after time how she may be led back to an appreciation of the softer charms of love and the home. Freedom is now the starting point; the social world in which these heroines move seems entirely different from the one occupied by the New Woman of the nineties. Mixed bathing, depicted with shocking suggestiveness in *Lord Ormont and His Aminta*, is *de rigueur* for the young in E. F. Benson's *Dodo the Second* (1914). Ann Veronica, peppering her speech with such expressions as 'damn!', 'ye gods!' and 'Lord!', would have been regarded by Gissing as irredeemably vulgar, but for Wells in 1909 is merely youthful and high-spirited. In E. V. Lucas's *Mr Ingleside* (1910), the heroine's desire to earn her own living provokes neither surprise nor opposition; indeed her father encourages her moves towards emancipation to the extent of obligingly inviting a suffragette to his home to see if this avenue of liberation might tempt his daughter. Everywhere there seems to be an amused indulgence of modernity; when in *Marriage* (1912) Wells introduces his dynamic young hero by making him crash his aeroplane on the heroine's croquet lawn, we have a neatly symbolic destruction of the old values which is continued in the rest of the novel. The word 'Victorian' itself became, with remarkable rapidity, a synonym for stuffy puritanism, outmoded propriety. 'I am not Victorian', announces one of the characters in *The Wife of Sir Isaac Harman*, establishing herself at once as fashionably broad-minded; and in the same novel the changes in attitude are proudly defined: 'We have done much in the last few years to destroy the severe limitations of Victorian delicacy, and all of us, from princesses and prime-ministers' wives downward, talk of topics that would have been considered quite gravely improper in the nineteenth century'.

But it was largely talk: when it came to action, the message for the post-Victorian liberated woman was clear and consistent – get back to the home. Heroines who flirt in the now fashionably approved manner with some of the New Woman's ideas are repeatedly brought by the end of the novel to confess their own femininity and to settle down with a man sufficiently strong to dominate even them. Whether it is his muscles or his forehead which bulge with unequivocal masculinity depends on the writer, but there is a general sense of relieved return to clearly defined sex roles. Thus in *Dodo the Second* the self-consciously 'advanced' heroine swaps her first fiancé, whose ideal of marital bliss is that 'I shall do embroidery in the evening, after dinner, while Nadine smokes', for an old-fashioned hero capable of snatching drowning maidens from rough seas. E. V. Lucas's Ann Ingleside turns down economic independence and the suffragettes in favour of the love of a good man. And Wells's Ann Veronica, who leaves home to take a degree in Biology at Imperial College and joins the suffragettes in parliament-storming raids, is brought in the end to express the prevailing wisdom about the new ideal of woman's place:

A woman wants a proper alliance with a man, a man who is better stuff than herself. She wants that and needs it more than anything else in the world. It may not be just, it may not be fair, but things are so. It isn't law, nor custom, nor masculine violence settled that. It is just how things happen to be. She wants to be free – she wants to be legally and economically free, so as not to be made subject to the wrong man; but only God, who made the world, can alter things to prevent her being slave to the right one. (*Ann Veronica*, ch.11)

The ideal is essentially the old one: woman's nature defines her place, in domestic surroundings with the right man at her side. But the New Woman influence directs that she should take up her position freely, protected by law, qualified to achieve financial independence and, perhaps more significantly, with a mature awareness of her own sexuality. These heroines are led back home by their men, but, particularly in Wells, amidst a welter of detailed analysis of their feelings about the relationship. Ann Veronica does not wait for Capes's divorce before living with him; the two scramble across the Alps together for several chapters, exchanging outbursts expressive of deep ecstasy and, we are told, taking measures to prevent the birth of illegitimate children before their union can be sealed with legal marriage. The recognition of female sexuality, which had seemed such a central part of the New Woman's struggle for emancipation, can now be easily assimilated into the old values. The new feminism was concerned almost entirely with the vote: as Wells's militant suffragette tells Sir Isaac Harman's wife 'we mustn't mix up Woman's Freedom with Matrimonial Cases'. To the New Woman of the nineties, such a statement would have appeared incomprehensible.

The new type of heroine was, then, sexually aware but domestically inclined. The feminist fervour of the nineties appears to have spread sufficiently widely into the popular consciousness to make potted versions of the New Woman's ideas a common part of a girl's youthful rebellion, a cheerful fling at old-fashioned convention before she settles down to become a thoroughly modern housewife. And the fact that it was the New Woman literature which had done it was freely acknowledged. Ann Veronica's distraught father accounts for his daughter's distressing behaviour with the observation that 'it's these damned novels. . . . These sham ideals and advanced notions, Women Who Dids, and all that kind of thing'. In *The Woman Movement* Ellen Key pays a handsome tribute to Victorian novelists: 'The truth about women in the century of women is found only in the impassioned books in which the hard struggles for freedom, work, or fame are recited'. And in 1911 the suffragette Swanhilde Bulan records the change in attitude to Ibsen's *A Doll's House*. Why, she wonders, had the play on its first appearance looked 'morbid', 'like an interesting bit of literature rather than . . . a bit of life'?

Of course! It is we who have changed. The fearless exposure of evil which we thought morbid in one playwright is courage when we see it done by a united band of women; the demand of Nora 'to her own life', which . . . we applauded with weak sympathy while agreeing that it was wholly impracticable, we now heartily commend. We come away from the play not puzzled and depressed as in old days, but cheerful and energetic.[5]

The Victorian heroines have done their job: the New Woman of the nineties, typically portrayed as engaged in a solitary struggle with an entirely hostile society, has become a part of the contemporary consciousness and so, perhaps, redundant.

The New Woman as a literary figure, then, slid from prominence with the whole apparatus of late Victorianism and became subsumed into the prevailing modern spirit. Many of her aims were forgotten, or deliberately rejected, as the suffrage struggle absorbed the feminist energies. But some of her achievements survived. The old stereotypes of the female character, with the strict moral divisions into what Charlotte Brontë had defined as 'angel' and 'fiend', were gone forever as female sexuality became a legitimate study for the novelist. The early twentieth-century heroine might have turned her back on the New Woman's pleas for personal freedom, but not on her analysis of physical responses. To portray sex in marriage was almost as great an achievement as to show it in free love, and moreover was an advance which could be developed steadily without inciting the shrieks of moral outrage which the New Woman writers had deliberately provoked. Feminist demands for freedom of expression, for smashing of taboos, had helped to drag the English novel out of its cocoon of stifling respectability and enabled it to confront aspects of female psychology and sexual behaviour which had previously been denied it. But ironically the main concerns of the New Woman novel achieved less lasting success than its incidental effects. Women were speedily packed off back to the home; ideas about free motherhood, sexual liberation or self-fulfilment through work were condemned to lie dormant for more than half a century before sprouting once more in the modern Women's Movement. As the hero's mother in H.G.Wells's *Marriage* sadly observes, the apparent liberation of the New Woman was fragile and ephemeral:

All the movement about us . . . women have become human beings. Woman's come out of being a slave, and yet she isn't an equal. . . . We've had a sort of sham emancipation, and we haven't yet come to the real one. (Book III, ch. 2)

The epitaph applies precisely to the Victorian New Woman: it remains to be seen if ultimately the same will be said of the modern one.

Notes

INTRODUCTION

1. *Woman*, 26 September 1894, p. 3. These lines were picked to win a readers' competition for the best definition of he New Woman.
2. R. Devereux ('A Woman of the Day'), 'The Feminine Potential', *Saturday Review*, 22 June 1895, pp. 824–5.
3. Matrimonial Causes Act, 1857, Section 27.
4. G. Drysdale, *The Elements of Science, or Physical, Sexual and Natural Religion*, 4th edn. (London, 1861) p. 355.
5. J. S. Mill, *The Subjection of Women*, (London, Everyman edn, 1965), p. 232.
6. Ibid, p. 273.
7. E. Lynn Linton, 'The Girl of the Period', *Saturday Review*, 14 March 1868, pp. 339–40.
8. S. Ellis, *The Daughters of England* (London, 1845) pp. 22–3.
9. E. R. Chapman, *Marriage Questions in Modern Fiction* (London, 1897), foreword.
10. R. le Gallienne, 'The New Womanhood', *Woman*, Literary Supplement, 2 May 1894, p. i.
11. These articles ran weekly in the *Saturday Review* from 18 May to 22 June 1895. They are reprinted, without the Rejoinders by 'Lady Jeune', in R. Devereux, *The Ascent of Woman* (London, 1896).
12. E. Lynn Linton, 'The Wild Women as Social Insurgents', *Nineteenth Century*, October 1891, pp. 596-605.
13. *Adult*, June 1897, pp. 1–2.
14. L. Harman, 'Pen Points', *Adult*, May 1898, p. 96.
15. H. E. M. Stutfield, 'The Psychology of Feminism', *Blackwood's Magazine*, January 1897, pp. 104–17.
16. 'The Silly Sexual Novel', *Woman*, Literary Supplement, 2 May 1894, pp. iii–iv.
17. 'A Century of Feminine Fiction', *All the Year Round*, 8 December 1894, pp. 537–40.
18. Ibid.

CHAPTER 1: MARRIAGE, MORALITY AND THE MODEL WOMAN

1. P. Coveney, *The Image of Childhood*, (London, Peregrine edn. 1967), pp. 179–84.
2. A. Pollard, *Mrs Gaskell: Novelist and Biographer* (Manchester, 1965), p. 88.

Notes

Notes

159

3. A. B. Hopkins, *Elizabeth Gaskell: Her Life and Work* (London, 1952), p. 124.
4. Pollard, op. cit., pp. 86–7.

CHAPTER 2: THE FICTION OF SEX AND THE NEW WOMAN

1. G. and W. Grossmith, *The Diary of a Nobody*, (London, Penguin edn, 1965), p. 89.
2. H. Ellis, *Women and Marriage* (London, 1888), p. 14.
3. T. Hardy, 'Candour in English Fiction', *New Review*, January 1890, pp. 15–21.
4. M. Oliphant, 'The Anti-Marriage League', *Blackwood's Magazine*, January 1896, pp. 135–49.
5. 'Past and Present Heroines in Fiction', *Saturday Review*, 28 July 1883, pp. 107–8.
6. See Introduction, note 15.
7. *Lloyd's Penny Weekly Miscellany*, iii (1844) p. 530. Quoted in M. Dalziel, *Popular Fiction 100 Years Ago* (London, 1957).
8. S. Grundy, *The New Woman* (London, 1894), p. 27.
9. 'A Chat with Mme Sarah Grand', *Woman*, Literary Supplement, 2 May 1894, pp. i–ii.
10. *Review of Reviews*, May 1893, pp. 543–5.
11. *Spectator*, 25 March 1893, p. 395.
12. *Critic*, 26 May 1894, pp. 353–4.
13. *Bookman*, November 1894, pp. 55–6.
14. *Nation*, 17 May 1894, pp. 369–70.
15. F. Harrison, *Funeral Address for Grant Allen* (privately printed, 1899).
16. G. Allen, 'Plain Words on the Woman Question', *Fortnightly Review*, October 1899, pp. 448–58.
17. E. Clodd, *Grant Allen, A Memoir* (London, 1900), pp. 165–6.
18. ' "Hill-Top" Novels and the Morality of Art', *Spectator*, 23 November 1895, pp. 722–4.
19. See Introduction, note 15.
20. T. de Vere White (ed.), *A Leaf from the Yellow Book* (London, 1958), p. 11.
21. J. L. May, *John Lane and the Nineties*, (London, 1936).
22. *Bookman*, December 1893, p. 87.
23. *Review of Reviews*, December 1893, p. 671.
24. *Athenaeum*, 13 April 1895, p. 470.
25. *Saturday Review*, 23 March 1895, pp. 383–4.
26. B. Leppington, 'Debrutalisation of Man', *Contemporary Review*, May 1895, pp. 725–43.
27. J. E. Hogarth, 'Literary Degenerates', *Fortnightly Review*, April 1895, pp. 586–92.
28. See Introduction, note 15.
29. *Athenaeum*, 3 October 1896, p. 448.

CHAPTER 3: THOMAS HARDY: NEW WOMEN FOR OLD

1. R. Y. Tyrrell, *Fortnightly Review*, June 1896, pp. 857–64.

2. E. Gosse, 'Thomas Hardy', *Speaker*, 13 September 1890, p. 295.

3. E. Slater, 'Men's Women in Fiction', *Westminster Review*, May 1898, pp. 571–7.

4. H. Ellis, 'Thomas Hardy's Novels', *Westminster Review*, April 1883, pp. 334–64.

5. *New Quarterly Magazine*, October 1879, pp. 412–31.

6. T. Hardy, 'The Tree of Knowledge', *New Review*, June 1894, p. 681.

7. Letter to Florence Henniker, 1 June 1896, F. E. Hardy and F. B. Pinion (eds.), *One Rare Fair Woman* (London, 1972), p. 51.

8. F. E. Hardy, *The Life of Thomas Hardy* (London, 1962), p. 220.

9. H. Quilter, *Spectator*, 3 February 1883, p. 154.

10. F. E. Hardy, op. cit., p. 271.

11. F. B. Pinion, *A Hardy Companion* (London, 1976), p. 44

12. For a fuller discussion of the dating of *The Woodlanders*, see D. Lodge's Introduction to the New Wessex Edition, (London, 1974).

13. Pinion, op. cit., p. 47.

14. M. Oliphant, *Blackwood's Magazine*, March 1892, pp. 464–74.

15. F. E. Hardy, op. cit., p. 271.

16. Unpublished notebook in the Dorset County Museum, 'Literary Notes II, 188–', January 31 1894.

17. Preface to the First Edition of *Jude the Obscure*, 1895.

18. F. E. Hardy, op. cit., p. 271.

19. R. Gittings, *Young Thomas Hardy* (London, 1975), pp. 94–5.

20. F. E. Hardy, op. cit., p. 272.

21. Unpublished letter to Mrs Fawcett, 30 November 1906, in the Fawcett Library.

22. *Pall Mall Gazette*, 12 November 1895, p. 107.

23. See note 4, Chapter 2.

24. *Athenaeum*, 24 November 1895, p. 709.

25. *Guardian*, 13 November 1895, p. 111.

26. See note 1, above.

27. *World*, 13 November 1895, p. 113.

28. A. J. Butler, 'Mr Hardy as a Decadent', *National Review*, May 1896, pp. 384–90.

29. *Critic*, 23 November 1895, p. 114.

30. D. F. Hannigan, *Westminster Review*, January 1896, pp. 136–9.

31. R. le Gallienne, *Idler*, February 1896, p. 137.

32. E. Gosse, *Cosmopolis*, January 1896, pp. 60–9. It will be noted that Gosse repeats the phrase – 'a sheaf of "purpose" stories on the "marriage question"'– which Hardy uses in his letter to Gosse of 10 November 1895 (F. E. Hardy, op. cit., p. 271). Although in this letter Hardy mentions having read Gosse's review, he must have been referring to an advance copy; and since it seems unlikely that Hardy would simply quote Gosse's remarks back at him, the probable explanation is that Gosse added Hardy's comments to his review before publication.

33. *Saturday Review*, 8 February 1896, pp. 153–4.

34. See note 14, above.

35. See note 24, above.

CHAPTER 4: MEREDITH AND GISSING: FAIR LADIES IN REVOLT AND ODD WOMEN

1. R. le Gallienne, *George Meredith: Some Characteristics* (London, 1890), p. 89.
2. *Bookman*, January 1896, pp. 127–8.
3. L. Housman, *Articles of Faith in the Freedom of Women* (London, 1911), p. 56.
4. F. Swinnerton, *George Gissing: A Critical Study* (London, 1924), p. 174.
5. *Spectator*, 11 August 1894, pp. 183–4.
6. R. C. McKay, 'George Gissing as a Portrayer of Society', in P. Coustillas (ed.), *Collected Articles on George Gissing* (London, 1968), p. 33.
7. Gissing's already poor health was, it seems, made considerably worse by the meagre meals served in the Fleury household.
8. Letter to Miss Price, 2 November 1888, C. L. Cline (ed.), *The Letters of George Meredith* (Oxford, 1970), Vol. II, p. 936.
9. 'The Marriage Handicap', *Daily Mail*, 24 September 1904, p. 5.
10. *Daily Telegraph*, 13 February 1908, p. 12.
11. See note 8, above.
12. *Spectator*, 25 January 1896, p. 137.
13. *Athenaeum*, 14 July 1894, pp. 55–6.
14. *Saturday Review*, 7 July 1894, pp. 18–19.
15. See note 3, Chapter 3.
16. Letter to Mrs Leslie Stephen, 19 May 1884, *Letters*, Vol. II, p. 737.
17. *Pall Mall Gazette*, 15 December 1884, p. 2.
18. Letter to Algernon Gissing, 14 February 1883, A. and E. Gissing (eds.), *Letters of George Gissing to Members of his Family* (London, 1927), p. 122.
19. Letter to Eduard Bertz, 2 June 1893, A. C. Young (ed.), *Letters of George Gissing to Eduard Bertz* (London, 1961), p. 171.
20. *Letters to his Family*, p. 225.
21. Letter to Bertz, 2 October 1894, *Letters to Bertz*, p. 188.
22. Bertz to Gissing, April 1897, *Letters to Bertz*, pp. 228–9.

CONCLUSION

1. E. Key, *The Woman Movement* (London, 1912), p. 24.
2. B. Winchester, 'The New Woman', *Arena*, April 1902, pp. 367–73.
3. Ibid.
4. L. Malet, 'The Threatened Re-Subjection of Women', *Fortnightly Review*, 1 May 1905, pp. 806–19.
5. S. Bulan, 'A Doll's House Revisited', *Votes for Women*, 17 February 1911, p. 8.

Bibliography

The following is a list of the editions consulted by the author, and from which the extracts cited in the text have been taken. The place of publication for books is London except where otherwise stated.

Allen, Grant, *The Woman Who Did* (1895)
—*The British Barbarians* (1895)
—*A Splendid Sin* (1896)
—*Miss Cayley's Adventures* (1899)
—'Plain Words on the Woman Question', *Fortnightly Review*, October 1889, 448–58
Austen, Jane, *The Novels of Jane Austen*, 6 vols ed. R. W. Chapman (Oxford, 1923–54)
Banks, J. A. and Olive, *Feminism and Family Planning in Victorian England* (Liverpool, 1964)
Barrie, J. M., 'Mr George Meredith's Novels', *Contemporary Review*, October 1888, 575–86
Barry, William, *The New Antigone*, 3 vols (1887)
Beaumont, Mary, *Two New Women* (1899)
Bennett, E. A., *Fame and Fiction: An Inquiry into Certain Popularities* (1901)
Benson, E. F., *Dodo: A Detail of the Day* (1893)
—*Dodo the Second* (1914)
Brontë, Charlotte, *Jane Eyre*, Everyman edition (1964)
—*Shirley*, Everyman edition (1964)
—*Villette*, Everyman edition (1964)
Brooke, Emma Frances, *A Superfluous Woman*, 3 vols (1894)
Burney, Fanny, *Evelina*, Oxford University Press edition (1968)
—*Camilla*, Oxford University Press edition (1972)
Caird, Mona, *The Wing of Azrael* (1889)
—*A Romance of the Moors* (Bristol, 1891)
—*The Daughters of Danaus* (1894)
—*The Morality of Marriage* (1897)
—*The Pathway of the Gods* (1898)

Carpenter, Edward, *Sex Love, and its Place in a Free Society* (Manchester, 1894)
—*Marriage in Free Society* (Manchester, 1894)
Chapman, E. R., *Marriage Questions in Modern Fiction* (1897)
Cline, C. L. (ed.), *The Letters of George Meredith*, 3 vols (Oxford, 1970)
Clodd, Edward, *Grant Allen, A Memoir* (1900)
Collis, J. S., *An Artist of Life: A Study of the Life and Work of Havelock Ellis* (1959)
Coustillas, Pierre (ed.), *The Letters of George Gissing to Gabrielle Fleury* (New York, 1964)
—*Collected Articles on George Gissing* (1966)
Coustillas, Pierre and Partridge, Colin (eds.), *Gissing: The Critical Heritage* (1972)
Coveney, Peter, *The Image of Childhood* (1967)
Cox, R. G. (ed.), *Thomas Hardy: The Critical Heritage* (1970)
Crow, Duncan, *The Victorian Woman* (1971)
Dalziel, Margaret, *Popular Fiction 100 Years Ago* (1957)
Davis, Oswald H., *George Gissing: A Study in Literary Leaning* (1966)
Devereux, R., *The Ascent of Woman* (1896)
Dickens, Charles, *Bleak House*, Oxford illustrated edition (1948)
—*Dombey and Son*, Oxford illustrated edition (1950)
—*Martin Chuzzlewit*, Oxford illustrated edition (1951)
Donnelly, M. C., *George Gissing: Grave Comedian* (Cambridge, Mass., 1954)
Dowie, Ménie Muriel, *A Girl in the Karpathians* (1891)
—*Gallia* (1895)
—*The Crook of the Bough* (1898)
Drysdale, George, *The Elements of Science, or Physical, Sexual and Natural Religion*, 4th ed. (1861)
Egerton, George (Mary Chavelita Dunne), *Keynotes* (1893)
—*Discords* (1894)
—*Symphonies* (1897)
—*Fantasias* (1898)
Eliot, George, *The Mill on the Floss*, Everyman (1966)
Ellis, Havelock, *Women and Marriage* (1888)
—*Studies in the Psychology of Sex*, Vol. VI, 'Sex in Relation to Society' (Philadelphia, 1911)
Ellis, Sarah, *The Daughters of England* (1845)
Gaskell, Elizabeth, *Ruth*, Everyman edition (1967)

Gettman, Royal A. (ed.), *George Gissing and H. G. Wells: Their Friendship and Correspondence* (1961)

Gissing, Algernon and Ellen (eds.), *Letters of George Gissing to Members of his Family* (1927)

Gissing, George, *Workers in the Dawn*, 3 vols (1880)

—*The Unclassed*, 3 vols (1884)

—*The Emancipated*, 3 vols (1890)

—*New Grub Street*, 3 vols (1891)

—*Born in Exile*, 3 vols (1892)

—*Denzil Quarrier* (1892)

—*The Odd Women*, 3 vols (1893)

—*In the Year of Jubilee* (1894)

—*The Paying Guest* (1895)

—*The Whirlpool* (1897)

—*The Town Traveller* (1898)

—*Our Friend the Charlatan* (1901)

Gittings, Robert, *Young Thomas Hardy* (1975)

Grand, Sarah, *Ideala* (1888)

—*The Heavenly Twins*, 3 vols (1893)

Grossmith, George and Weedon, *The Diary of a Nobody*, Penguin edition (1965)

Grundy, Sydney, *The New Woman* (1894)

Hammerton, J. A., *George Meredith in Anecdote and Criticism* (1909)

Hansson, L. M. (trans. Hermione Ramsden), *Modern Woman* (1896)

—*We Women and Our Authors* (1899)

Hardy, Evelyn (ed.), *Thomas Hardy's Notebooks*

Hardy, Evelyn and Gittings, Robert (eds.), *Emma Hardy, Some Recollections* (1961)

Hardy, Evelyn and Pinion, F. B. (eds.), *One Rare Fair Woman* (1972)

Hardy, Florence Emily, *The Life of Thomas Hardy* (1962)

Hardy, Thomas, *Complete Novels*, The Wessex Edition (1912)

Harrison, Frederic, *Funeral Address for Grant Allen*, (Privately printed, 1899)

Hogarth, Janet E., 'Literary Degenerates', *Fortnightly Review*, April 1895, 586–92

Hopkins, A. B., *Elizabeth Gaskell: Her Life and Work* (1952)

Houghton, Walter E., *The Victorian Frame of Mind* (1957)

Housman, Lawrence, *Articles of Faith in the Freedom of Women* (1911)

Ibsen, Henrik, *Hedda Gabler*, Penguin edition (1961)

—*Ghosts*, Penguin edition (1964)

—*A Doll's House*, Penguin edition (1965)

Iota (Mrs Mannington Caffyn), *A Yellow Aster*, 3 vols (1894)
—*Children of Circumstance*, 3 vols (1894)
—*A Quaker Grandmother* (1896)
Jackson, Holbrook *The Eighteen Nineties* (1913)
Kelvin, Norman, *A Troubled Eden: Nature and Society in the Works of George Meredith* (1961)
Key, Ellen, (trans. Arthur G. Chater), *Love and Marriage* (1911)
Key, Ellen (trans. M. B. Borthwick), *The Woman Movement* (1912)
Korg, Jacob, *George Gissing: A Critical Biography* (1965)
Latey, William (ed.), *The Matrimonial Causes Act* (1937)
Lee, G. S., 'The Sex-Conscious School in Fiction', *New World*, March 1900, 77–84
Le Gallienne, Richard, *George Meredith: Some Characteristics* (1890)
Leppington, Blanche, 'Debrutalisation of Man', *Contemporary Review*, May 1895, 725–43
Lerner, L. and Holmstrom, J. (eds.), *Thomas Hardy and his Readers* (1967)
Linton, E. Lynn, 'The Girl of the Period', *Saturday Review*, 14 March 1868, 339–40
—'The Wild Women as Social Insurgents', *Nineteenth Century*, October 1891, 596–605
Lucas, E. V., *Mr Ingleside* (1910)
Malet, Lucas, 'The Threatened Re-subjection of Women', *Fortnightly Review*, May 1905, 806–19
May, J. Lewis, *John Lane and the Nineties* (1936)
Meredith, George, The Memorial Edition (1909–11)
Merrick, Marie, 'The Woman of the Period', *Arena*, February 1903, 161–66
Mill, J. S., *The Subjection of Women*, Everyman edition (1965)
Mitchell, David, *The Fighting Pankhursts* (1967)
Montefiore, Dora B., *From a Victorian to a Modern* (1927)
Murdoch, W. G. Blaikie, *The Renaissance of the Nineties* (1911)
Nordau, Max, *Degeneration* (1895)
Oliphant, M., 'The Anti-Marriage League', *Blackwood's Magazine*, January 1896, 139–49
Orel, H. (ed.), *Thomas Hardy's Personal Writings* (1967)
Pearsall, Ronald, *The Worm in the Bud*, (1971)
Peel, Robert, *The Creed of a Victorian Pagan* (Cambridge, Mass., 1931)
Pinion, F. B., *A Hardy Companion* (1968)

Pollard, Arthur, *Mrs Gaskell: Novelist and Biographer* (Manchester, 1965)

Poole, Adrian, *Gissing in Context* (1975)

Priestley, J. B., *George Meredith* (1927)

Pritchett, V. S., *George Meredith and English Comedy* (1970)

Roberts, Morley, *The Private Papers of Henry Maitland* (1923)

Rover, Constance, *Love, Morals and the Feminists* (1970)

Schreiner, Olive, *The Story of an African Farm*, 3 vols (1883)

Sergeant, Adeline, 'George Meredith's Views of Women', *Temple Bar*, June 1889, 411–25

Shore, Arabella, 'The Novels of George Meredith', *British Quarterly Review*, April 1897, 411–25

Slater, Edith, 'Men's Women in Fiction', *Westminster Review*, May 1898, 571–7

Smith, G., 'The Women of George Meredith', *Fortnightly Review*, May 1896, 775–90

Smith, T. R. (ed.), *The Woman Question* (New York, 1918)

Strachey, Ray, '*The Cause*'. *A Short History of the Women's Movement in Great Britain* (1928)

Stutfield, Hugh E. M., 'The Psychology of Feminism', *Blackwood's Magazine*, January 1897, 104–17

Swinnerton, Frank, *George Gissing: A Critical Study* (1924)

Thackeray, W. M., *Vanity Fair*, Penguin edition (1968)

Thomson, Patricia, *The Victorian Heroine: A Changing Ideal* (1956)

Tindall, Gillian, *The Born Exile: George Gissing* (1974)

Trollope, Anthony, *Can You Forgive Her?*, (Oxford, 1973)

Wagner, Geoffrey, *Five for Freedom: A Study of Feminism in Fiction* (1972)

Weber, Carl J. (ed.), '*Dearest Emmie*': *Thomas Hardy's Letters to his First Wife* (1963)

Wells, H. G., *Ann Veronica* (1909)

—*Marriage* (1912)

—*The Wife of Sir Isaac Harman* (1914)

White, Terence de Vere (ed.), *A Leaf from the Yellow Book: The Correspondence of George Egerton* (1958)

Winchester, Boyd, 'The New Woman', *Arena*, April 1902, 367–73

Winston, Ella W., 'Foibles of the New Woman', *Forum*, April 1896, 196–2

Wollstonecraft, Mary, *A Vindication of the Rights of Woman*, Everyman edition (1965)

Wood, Mrs Henry, *East Lynne* (1861)

Woods, Alice, *George Meredith as Champion of Women and of Progressive Education* (Oxford, 1937)

Wright, Walter F., *Art and Substance in George Meredith* (Lincoln, Nebraska, 1953)

Yates, May, *George Gissing: An Appreciation* (1922)

Yonge, Charlotte, *The Clever Woman of the Family*, Collected Works, Vol. X (1880)

Young, Arthur C. (ed.), *The Letters of George Gissing to Eduard Bertz 1887–1903* (1961)

Index